troika®

63-83

Ben Harris and Lawrence Illsley

Troika 63 – 83

ISBN 978-0-9574873-0-7

Written and edited by Ben Harris and Lawrence Illsley.

Published by It's pronounced 'Aitch'.
For more copies of this book or further information, please email: info@troikapedia.co.uk

Typeset and designed by Amy Willoughby.
Printed and bound in Great Britain.

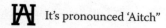 It's pronounced 'Aitch"

In memory of Alan Brough

From left to right:
Kristen Roth, Benny Sirota, Stella Benjamin, Leslie Illsley
Photograph courtesy of Judith Illsley

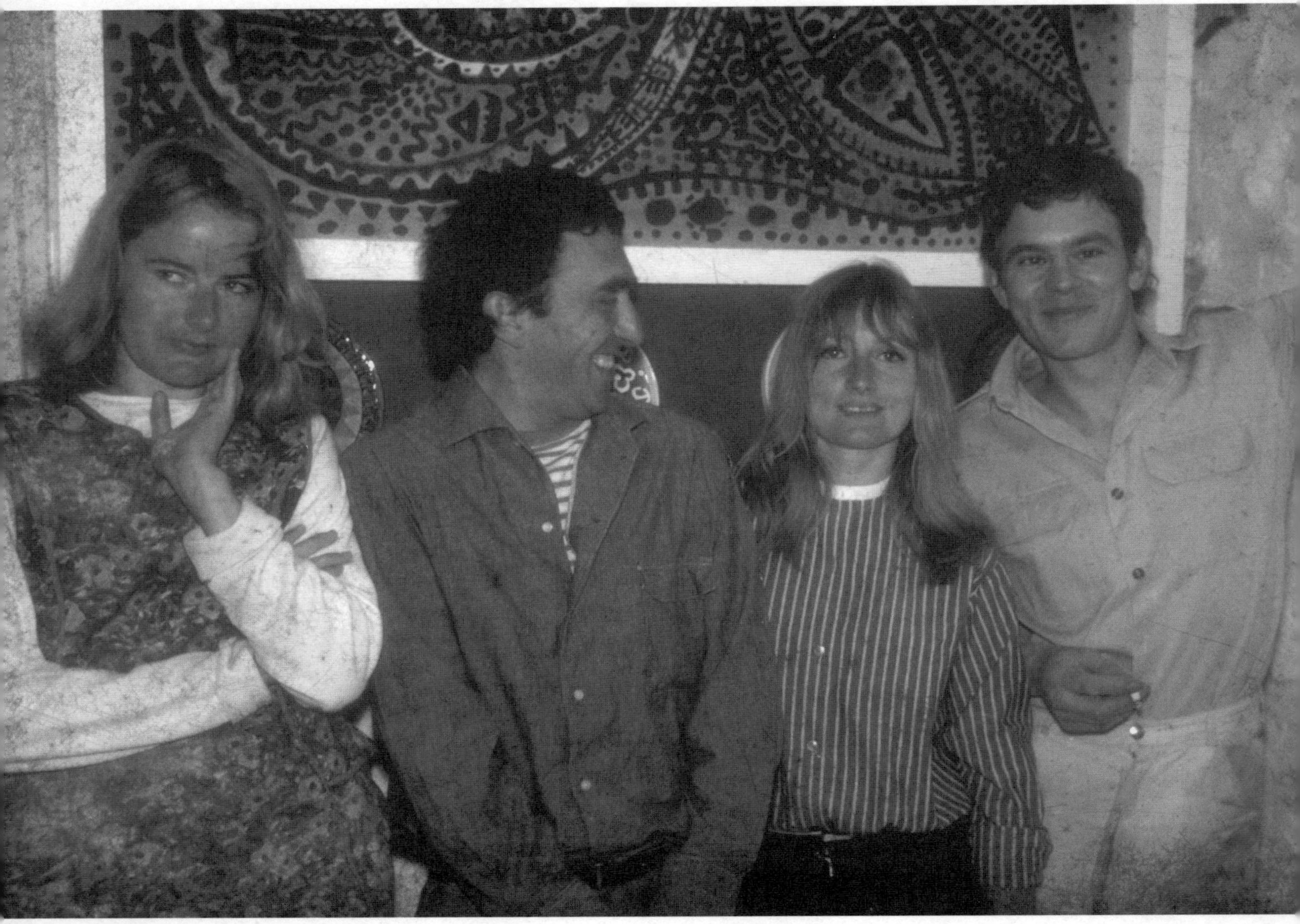

We would like to thank...

Judith Illsley and Rachael Illsley for everything, including food, warmth, use of their Troika archive and deep debate. Benny Sirota and the Sirota family, Jacqui, Theo and Sophie for their help and hospitality. Thank you to Bryan Illsley for providing such crucial insight into his brother.

The former employees of Troika for their time and memories:
Avril Machray, Jane Parsons, Roland Bence, John Bedding, Louise McClary, Sylvia Balcombe, Julian Greenwood-Penny, Stella Benjamin, Sarah Watson, Penny Dass, Ruth Larratt, Simone Kilburn, Honor Nankervis and Kristen Nesbitt. Also to Alan and Sheila Brough, Maggie Fisher and Maria Heital.

Theo Sirota for taking the photographs of his father's collection and for moving heaven and earth to get those pictures to us.

Richard Wheatley for allowing us into his home to take pictures of his collection.

Colin Richards and Teresa Bretherton for all their support and for allowing us to use their pictures of their collection.

Paul Longthorne for allowing us into the Market Place Gallery, Marazion many, many times.

Alison Bevan, Katie Herbert and everyone at Penlee House Gallery, Penzance for believing we could work to a deadline.

Jean White for proof-reading and for not letting us get away with anything. Becky Boley and Shelley Knowles-Dixon for their additional proof-reading.

Amy Willoughby for the design and photography.

To our friends for putting up with our continuous debate when we should have been socialising.

Special thanks to Shelley Knowles-Dixon and Amy Willoughby for their continuous support.

Ben Harris

Ben Harris was born in Truro, Cornwall in 1981. Ambition took him to London in 2001 where he pursued a professional music career to some success. He has a profound interest in the obscure and has been a Troika collector and researcher for a number of years. He now works as an assistant film editor and documentarian. He lives in West London.

Lawrence Illsley

Lawrence Illsley is a writer and a musician. His first book was published by Proverse Publishing and is an epic poem called Astra and Sebastian. He is a singer-songwriter and the Musical Director of the theatre company Sparkle and Dark's Travelling Players (www.sparkleanddark.com). He teaches maths in the evenings and is studying for a degree in Psychology with the Open University. He lives in north London with his fiancé Shelley Knowles-Dixon.

Contents

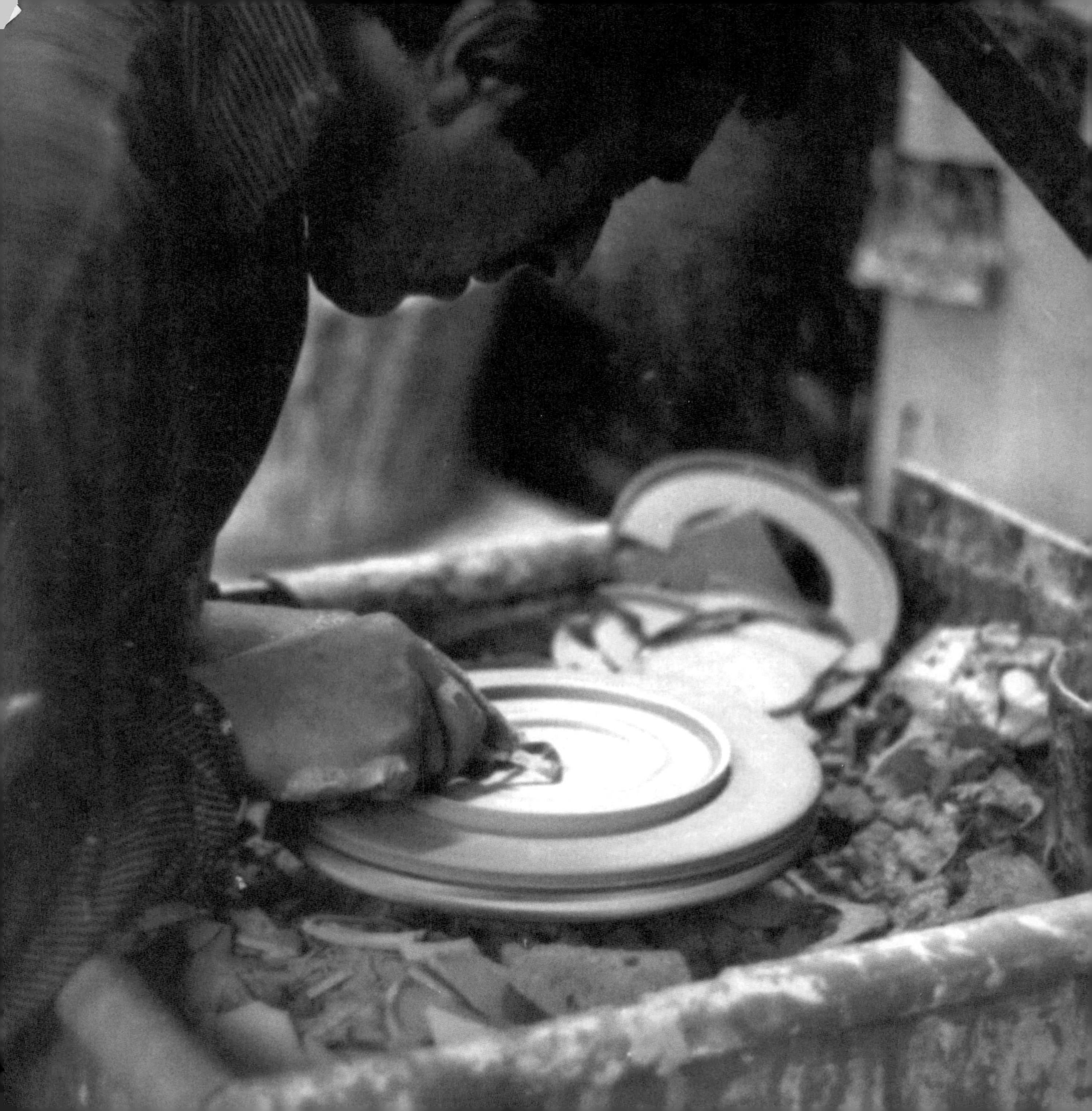

As we mark the fiftieth anniversary of Troika's opening, it is the perfect time to discover the personal stories of the people that made Troika successful and to construct a coherent time-line for its history and output. Seventeen former employees have been interviewed; their memories form the basis for this book.

New facts, and primary evidence in the form of photographs and documents that have not been published before, have been included, which help define the story and give a greater insight into the running of Troika and its contribution to the British art scene.

'Troika 63-83' contains reasoned arguments as to why Troika should be reclassified as 'art' and explores this in great detail. Set up by potter Benny Sirota and sculptor Leslie Illsey, Troika's output changed over time from functional craft objects to conceptual stand-alone pieces of sculpture, extending the ideas and practise of sculpture into the medium of clay. The use of clay at Troika meant they, as artists, had access to a medium of creation. By mass producing their output, they were able to allow more people access to the ownership of art objects.

'Troika 63-83' will explore how Troika became part of a wave of social and artistic change in order to better understand the nature of their work and what they achieved. However, it is beyond the scope of this book to provide an in-depth critical analysis of their work. It is hoped the comparisons and insights offered will inspire others to reassess Troika's work in order to fully understand the extent of their achievements.

Instead, the book will focus its attempt to understand their contribution to history by exploring the personal motives of the two partners and the people that worked there. Through these motivations we can begin to understand Troika's practice and choice of medium and also why Troika's work looks and feels unique.

Although it is easy to see Benny and Leslie alone as the force which moulded Troika's journey through two decades, it is important to recognise the others who influenced their history. To see Troika as a group we also need to understand the contributions made by those people who joined the collective; the casters, fettlers, decorators, and those who bought the work they produced.

What follows is their story.

Chapter One

"Do you know how the name Troika came about? It's to do with my grandfather. Perhaps this is mythology, but my grandfather and his wife escaped from Russia, he escaped dressed as a woman, on a troika; a sledge with three horses. Then of course there were three of us and it gelled."

– Benny Sirota

The train tracks stop because there is nowhere else to go, only the sea. Many people have found St Ives in this way. They found the slipway leading up from the walled harbour where multi-coloured fishing boats bob easily on the lapping tide.

The summer would attract thronging crowds but these pleasure-seekers would have left by September. Only a few stayed to brave the winter; those who had nothing to go back to. Those who stayed needed something to keep them there at the end of the line.

Amongst the travellers were people of substance. People for whom life was more than the journey, people for whom life was creation. These were the artists and it was to be the artists who would stay through the winter to work. This made St Ives a town in transition. Old trades were dying out; fishing and mining were already becoming just tales to scare the young folk with.

Migration to St Ives wasn't new; Bernard Leach had arrived in 1920 via Japan. Barbara Hepworth and Ben Nicholson had arrived from London in the forties. For over twenty years these artists and their contemporaries had been dominating the landscape by evoking it in pottery, paint and sculpture.

Benny Sirota had first arrived in 1948 with his then girlfriend Wendy. She wanted to study with Bernard Leach. In order to support her Benny worked for local businessman Ivor 'Pop' Short in his restaurant the Copper Kettle. They lived in a tent on the headland for nearly three years but never made enough to fund her dream. In 1951 they left for London to join the wave of excitement surrounding the Festival of Great Britain.

Benny had a taste for St Ives. In 1962 he returned with his new girlfriend, Stella Benjamin, his good friend Daphne Wells and her new boyfriend. They sailed down from London, stopping in Cowes for a whole week to wait for a storm to pass. Daphne co-owned the Powell and Wells pottery, which was based in London and was relocating to St Ives. They were all looking for a new life and this time Benny meant to build something more sustainable.

Leslie Illsley had just arrived with his new wife Caroline. They had both recently graduated from art school in London and wanted to paint. Their first trip to Cornwall was to see Leslie's artist brother, Bryan Illsley who was living in Helston. Whilst exploring the peninsula they fell in love with St Ives and would only return to London to fetch their belongings. Caroline's family were very well off. Her mother, the artist Peggy Frank, was so taken with the idea of St Ives she bought two houses there. One for the young couple and the house next door for herself.

Benny and Leslie met at the end of 1962 in the Sloop Pub. With barstools rocking on the slate flagstones and surrounded by fisherman, these two young and restless men got to know each other over several pints of Bass. Benny had an interest in pottery which had flourished whilst working with Dougie Zadek at Cobham Pottery in Surrey. Leslie was an establishing sculptor and painter. Naturally, the conversation turned to art. They talked of the painters they loved, of Klee, Mondrian, Cezanne, Klimpt and sculptors like Brancusi and Modigliani. They talked about the local scene and the studio potters. Benny had an admiration for tradition but Leslie abhorred it. He thought that the whole country, let alone the town, needed shaking up. Benny remembers talking to Leslie,

"We started talking about pottery and Bernard Leach and all the sort of things that were going on and how there was need for something different and I agreed with him. I don't know if either of us knew what that difference was."

The two men instantly got along. Many who had been called to St Ives had found like-minded souls. It was part of the magic of the place.

Whilst in London working, Leslie had studied part time at St Martin's College of Art. When he finished his course he was enamoured with modernism, free-thinking, and politics. He was an angry young man, angry at the establishment and at the lack of opportunity for those in the poorer classes like himself. Benny was always less angry than Leslie. He was a bit older and perhaps more self-assured but not unsympathetic to these issues.

There was a definite change in attitude from the fifties to the sixties; the new educated youth had begun to break away from tradition. In St Ives the local Cornish fishermen and Methodist community resented the intrusion of the wave of travellers who brought modern ideas with them. But the tide was turning against those who had dragged a town up out of the raging sea. The ideas Benny and Leslie were describing to each other were to be the future. Change is often not wrought easily but they didn't expect any help; they were simply going to build it themselves.

With this ethos Benny's friend Daphne Wells was busy converting a room in a warehouse into a pottery. Her business, Powell and Wells, was a commercial pottery founded by herself and Elizabeth Powell. They had successfully managed to make hand-painted bedroom name signs and tiles for years in Chelsea, London. They made small perfume bottles and door

"In the back of a mini in the snow ...we arrived in St Ives and it was fantastic, it was heaven. I woke up and saw these seagulls, and the light, you don't notice it until you go away."

Kristen Roth

handles that were formed from two-piece moulds. The pottery employed a few decorators to hand paint these tiles, including a young artist called Kristen Roth.

In the autumn of 1962 Daphne had become frustrated with London and decided to move the operation to St Ives. Before he moved back permanently, Benny had been regularly visiting St Ives and had found Daphne the ideal premises in a small cul-de-sac called Wheal Dream. It was a building owned by 'Pop' Short, his former employer at the Copper Kettle in 1948. The cul-de-sac nestled at the bottom of a grass-covered, chapel-topped hill called The Island that splits St Ives in half, the harbour on one side and Porthminster Beach on the other.

Benny had become good friends with Daphne when they met in Earls Court in the 50's; she introduced him to a whole new world of jazz, classical music, art and literature,

"I don't think I even had a radio in those days, it opened my eyes. When you haven't had any education and you suddenly get aware of things you are like a sponge. I mean it was 'wow'."

After settling in, Daphne went to fetch Kristen from London and drove her down to St Ives so she could continue decorating for them. Once the move was complete Benny's girlfriend, Stella, was also given a job at the pottery as a decorator, Benny remembers, "They taught her how to decorate, they made tiles. There were oblong ones and there were square ones and ones with pink flowers in the corner. Oh and they made door knobs, with ducks on them, beautifully painted." Stella humorously remembers these pieces as, "Those bloody tiles".

Kristen remembers her first impression of St Ives,

"I was about 18 and had just come over from South Africa. I went to Art College there. When Daphne decided to move to Cornwall she took me with her, I was the only worker who went with her. In the back of a mini in the snow and we arrived in St Ives and it was fantastic, it was heaven. I woke up and saw these seagulls, and the light, you don't notice it until you go away. It was very quiet when I was there. Lots of potters, there were ten I knew... It was so quiet in the winter. We didn't have all the restaurants we had fish and chips. There was an old guy who used to sell vegetables down by the quay with his pony and trap and there was another guy who used to come into the pub with his dog and give his dog half a pint of bitter. There were real local people, fishermen."

After only a few months, the atmosphere had changed at Powell and Wells. Daphne was not satisfied with her new environment and wanted to move to America with her boyfriend but had recently signed a five-year lease on Christmas Day 1962.

Benny saw an opportunity in Daphne's predicament. He had been looking for premises to convert into a pottery for a few months and had recently failed to buy a row of cottages in Zennor. He approached Leslie with an audacious plan; the takeover of the Powell and Wells tile business. Leslie was not particularly keen to become a potter but saw the potential. The idea developed that maybe they would make tiles by day and could use the space in the evening as an art studio. Leslie really wanted a space to continue sculpting. He had applied for a space at the 'old net lofts' in St Ives which had been used by painters since the 1880's. The owners were not interested in renting to a sculptor and so turned him down. Leslie was happy enough painting for free in the house he shared with Caroline but in order to sculpt, greater space was needed.

Even with the promise of a studio Leslie didn't take the business plan seriously at first. Leslie and his wife Caroline were not in St Ives to set up a business, they were there to live the artistic dream. They moved there not to be tied down but to be free. The couple had already planned to hitch-hike to Ibiza for the winter to paint. In their house on Island Road they had created a pop-up art gallery and sandwich shop. Over the summer they had been selling coffee, sandwiches and paintings out of their kitchen window. Without needing to pay rent on the building, they had made enough money from the tourists and surfers who meandered past the house to fund their plan to disappear from the desolate St Ives winter for some fun. They left in the autumn of 1962.

Benny on the other hand had been trying to start a new business for a few years. He had previously run a lithographic printing business in Old Compton Street called Dittograph. He was a few years older than Leslie and wanted something stable of his own. After Leslie left for Ibiza Benny, in order to keep his dream of starting a pottery alive, went to work for Daphne to learn how the business was run and how the tiles were made. It was a valuable decision. Leslie returned earlier than expected from Ibiza. Caroline had become pregnant and wanted to have the baby in St Ives supported by her mother who lived in the house next door.

When he discovered that Leslie was back in St Ives, Benny immediately went to see him. He was attracted by Leslie's spontaneity and personality and saw in him a valuable partner for his enterprise. Leslie now took Benny's plan much more seriously. With a baby on the way a reliable source of income was needed. It wouldn't be enough to rely upon the sporadic income from the sale of a few sandwiches and paintings. Impromptu trips to artistic communities like Ibiza were also out of the window. He was being forced to grow up.

Now Leslie and Benny had committed to each other, they needed to find a third partner to join them on their venture as they couldn't raise the capital to buy the business on their own. They soon met a young architect called Jan Thompson in the Sloop and spoke passionately about their new business venture. They talked not only of their immediate plans to continue manufacturing tiles, as Powell and Wells had been doing, but also about future plans to expand into interior design and ceramics for domestic use. They began to talk about a design studio inspired by the modern, sharp designs coming out of Scandinavia. Leslie was well aware of this type of design having lived in Scandinavia in the late 50's. He was forced to leave when the girl he was with pulled a knife on him. He beat a hasty retreat back to Kingston-upon-Thames, Surrey, where he met Caroline.

Jan was also familiar with these design concepts and was excited to hear that young British artists were inspired by them. Based upon function and economy, yet indulging in smooth glazes, sharp edges and geometric designs, they offered the ultimate modern alternative to the drab austerity of 50's Britain. It was the antithesis of Bernhard Leach. From reaction came inspiration.

It was also suggested that they could make architectural detailing for houses. Following the trend in London for reliefs and sculptures incorporated into the walls and plans of houses, akin to some works by the sculptor Henry Moore.

Jan was convinced. This new business seemed perfect for a young aspiring architect to invest in. He felt the excitement, saw the promise and most importantly put his money where his mouth was. He spoke to the bank and was told he could borrow a thousand pounds if his father acted as guarantor.

Jan was keen to focus on his burgeoning career in architecture which suited Leslie and Benny perfectly. They only needed a silent partner. A third powerful voice may have taken the project over the edge. The unfortunate end to many a communal dream.

Now it was up to Benny and Leslie to match him. Leslie borrowed a thousand pounds from Caroline's father, a wealthy barrister. Benny didn't have any money yet,

"I asked my mother, I didn't ask her for a loan but I went to see the bank, because they saw the figures from Powell and Wells and said well if you can get a guarantor for the money we'll lend it to you. So my mother guaranteed it, so that's how I got my thousand. So I didn't actually have to ask her for the cash."

On the 26th day of March 1963 they went to a local solicitors and an impressive legal document was spread on the table before them. It was huge, about A2 size and written in an archaic calligraphy with some sections highlighted in red ink. Quite beautiful in its own way but it couldn't have represented the crumbling fortress of the old Britain better if it tried. With a wry smile the three partners dutifully signed this document. This, with the addition of a letter signed by 'Pop' Short releasing Daphne from the agreement, allowed the Powell and Wells pottery to be taken on by the three new partners.

Daphne Wells' lease was originally for five years. It set the rent at £104 per year for the first three years and £208 thereafter. It also allowed a sign to be affixed to the building. The sale transferred the remainder of the original five-year lease, the goodwill, premises, fixtures, fittings and trade utensils, including the potters' kilns and one potter's wheel to the new partners, for the princely sum of £1500. By signing this agreement they not only secured a place but the whole business, "contracts, engagements, benefits and advantage" so, order book and all. A clause stated that Daphne was not allowed to open a similar business for at least three years. It also stated that if the pottery was to make more than £4000 gross by the end of its first tax year they would have to pay an extra £500 to Daphne. Now they needed an identity. Benny explains how they came to the name,

"Do you know how the name Troika came about? It's to do with my grandfather. Perhaps this is mythology, but my grandfather and his wife escaped from Russia, he escaped dressed as a woman, on a troika, a sledge with three horses. Then of course there were three of us and it gelled."

The name also appealed because of its angular letters and sound. It seemed to predict the type of work they wanted to produce.

With everything in place they went to look at the building as the new proprietors. It was hardly a studio, more a small dark room on the ground floor of a large warehouse. As a working building it was not finished or made inviting in any way. Kristen described it as like a cavern, "It had a dirt floor. It was like a big cave." The walls were just whitewashed granite, peeling and lumpy. The door was under the outside steps that led up to the Seaman's Mission. Next door to them downstairs was a milk distributor, which Benny remembers it often stinking of sour milk.

Despite the surroundings business was continuing as normal. Daphne's employees, Stella and Kristen, simply stayed at their benches as the ownership changed. Benny kept filling up

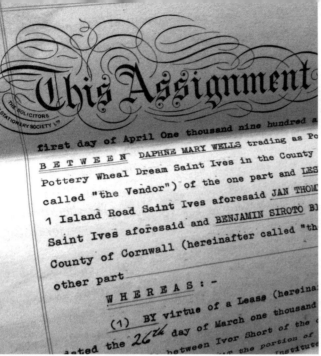
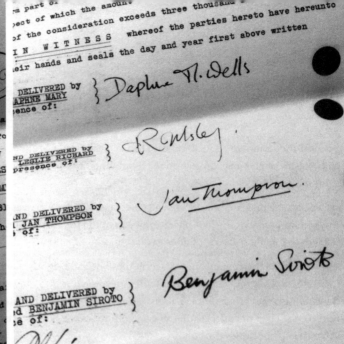

Contract transferring ownership of Powell and Wells, signed by Daphne, Leslie, Jan and Benny

the little kiln in the corner and watched over the firing. Only a small kiln was needed because the products they were making were all stackable. The only difference was that Leslie now came to work in the mornings too.

There was an order book which needed to be filled. Benny and Leslie planned to fulfil the commercial obligations of Powell and Wells and keep producing tiles. According to Benny there was a "guy in Scotland who was selling thousands of pounds worth of products". This would allow all of them to earn a decent living and Jan some extra money in addition to his architecture business. Benny stated quite vehemently,

   "There was a business plan. Well there was! One of the things I said to Leslie fairly early was that we needed a business plan. We ran a tile business first!"

In the beginning earning a living was at the core of Troika and fitted in with the partners' socialist values. By taking over a business they could provide themselves with the means to pursue their own artistic ambitions in their spare time. They would support themselves, never needing to be supported by a benefactor. Both partners wanted the freedom to choose their own destiny. This was the defining factor not only of Benny and Leslie's life choices but of that era as a whole. The whole project was undertaken with the fearless confidence of that unique time in history; the confidence of youth. All over the country young people were making the world in their own image. As Stella recalls, "It was quite exciting at the time. Three people getting together and deciding to go for it."

Soon after they had moved in at Wheal Dream, Leslie and Caroline's daughter was born in May. Leslie had a huge admiration for Rembrandt and so she was named Saskia after Rembrandt's wife.

The fact that the building was in such a state made it a blank canvas to these young artists. Benny remembers that the first big change was to tile the earth floor. "We bought all these other tiles but made some extra ones to fill it in, a bit of colour."

They covered the floor mainly in terracotta tiles but laid brightly painted tiles in a pattern between these. Everyone got a chance to design some tiles, which were painted with designs of flowers, suns and other simple patterns. You could still see them today if the council were to remove the layer of concrete on the ground floor of the St Ives Museum, the institution which currently occupies the building.

They put up shelves by the entrance way, partitioning off the workspace and creating a showroom in which to display their work. Then, as stated in the contract they put up a sign, the pillar outside the door had the word 'TROIKA' emblazoned vertically down it in coloured mosaic tiles. They didn't stop with the sign but changed the whole side of the building as Benny recalls, "We put a front in and built a plinth. I nearly got killed over that plinth."

Benny tells a particularly nasty story about how he was threatened with a knife and told to leave the area because it was felt that the new 'outsiders' were ruining the town. The locals weren't entirely happy with the changing of the landscape that had been familiar for decades.

The plinth had coloured Troika tiles embedded in its side, Benny remembers that years later, "All those tiles got pinched." This seems remarkably in keeping with the tradition where Cornish farmhouses were made from granite 'borrowed' from ancient monuments. The only tile visible today is embedded in the floor outside of the fire exit of the museum.

Bryan, Leslie's brother made them some posters and a sign which they put up on the outside of 3 Seaview Place encouraging people towards their secluded business, urging them to explore something new. They were promptly told to take it down by the staid, world-wary townsfolk. They had arrived.

Their studio at Wheal Dream was tiny and dusty from the clay, there was no fan or ventilation and everyone was chain-smoking. At the end of the day the four of them would emerge from the gloom taking in gulps of the blustery sea air, whilst covered in clay and chemicals. It was a dirty job but unusual and in an exciting place at an exciting time.

"It was quite exciting at the time. Three people getting together and deciding to go for it."
Stella Benjamin

Benny Sirota at Wheal Dream, St Ives

Items on display; Troika showroom, Wheal Dream, St Ives, Cornwall

St Ives was establishing itself as the largest and most important art colony outside of London. The town was alive. Stella's story is typical of the time; she describes leaving school at 15,

"I wanted to go to art school but my dad said 'no you have to get a job'. So I worked in insurance for 5 years. But I thought I have to change my life. So I got into the Regent Poly. I didn't want to take any exams, do the NDD or do any courses. I just wanted to be there to soak up the atmosphere. Patrick Millard the Head said 'what do you want to do? Do you want to do the NDD?' I said 'no'. 'Do you want to be a teacher?' I said 'no'. I said 'I just want to be here'. And that was the truth. I just wanted to get out of that office and do something different. I had to work I didn't have a grant. I worked in cinemas, shoe shops, newsagents, wherever. Of course there were jobs, you could be an usherette with the ice-cream tray. They don't have those any more."

In the culmination to this radical change to her life, Stella had travelled down to St Ives and was now employed as an artist and surrounded by them. Wheal Dream itself even had some artistic provenance. Painter Trevor Bell, who sold Benny his first 'real' painting and sculptor Brian Wall had shared a studio there.

"You were surrounded by artists, it was on your doorstep, you knew all the artists. Peter Lanyon, Patrick Heron, Johnny Wells and Willie Barns-Graham, Barbara Hepworth, Bernard Leach, they were all around. Penwith (gallery) was still going; it was quite an important place showing all those people. It was there and you did talk about it sometimes, amongst other things."

They were all wanderers that had found a home. The same was true for Kristen, "I wandered to St Ives. Most people wandered down there. It was not just potters it was writers and painters. All escaping. I don't think they would have done all that in London. You just sort of end up there.

"You had to be quite tough really. You could quite easily get sucked into it. Too much pot or things like that. There was a lot about. But it was all at parties. It was a very creative place."
Kristen Roth

The Sloop Pub as it is today, St Ives, Cornwall

I ran away from home, for a good reason. I was safe in St Ives because we were all the same sort of people. We were a community. We weren't lost, we just buggered about a lot, looked after each other. It was lovely, like going home. Finding like-minded people. And there were always jobs. If this didn't work you could get a job doing something else. You were never restricted. There was a lot of freedom."

It wasn't all work; Kristen said how easy it was to get caught up in the party scene. It was easy to get hold of drugs; perhaps not the range available to your average college kid today but cannabis was plentiful, "You had to be quite tough really. You could quite easily get sucked into it. Too much pot or things like that. There was a lot about. But it was all at parties. It was a very creative place."

Outside The Sloop was the focus of the town's discontent. The beatniks sat on the wall by the slipway. There was concern that they would impede the launching of the lifeboat which had to be towed along the harbour front, from the lifeboat house to the slipway.

The word beatnik was hot on every tongue. The artists were often confused with the beatniks. Stella remembers the ill feeling towards anyone that was not local, "We were all beatniks. We had long hair. I was told to cut it. The town was very Cornish, anti-beatniks, no undesirables! They were all beatniks you see. All the pubs had signs on the doors saying no beatniks. Beatniks sitting on the railings. Bloody beatniks coming down every year. They took the railings down to stop them sitting there."

Inside The Sloop was where the two worlds collided. Local fishermen and artists would finish their day's work at the bar and it was here that Troika found a home.

Inside Troika studio, St Ives, Cornwall

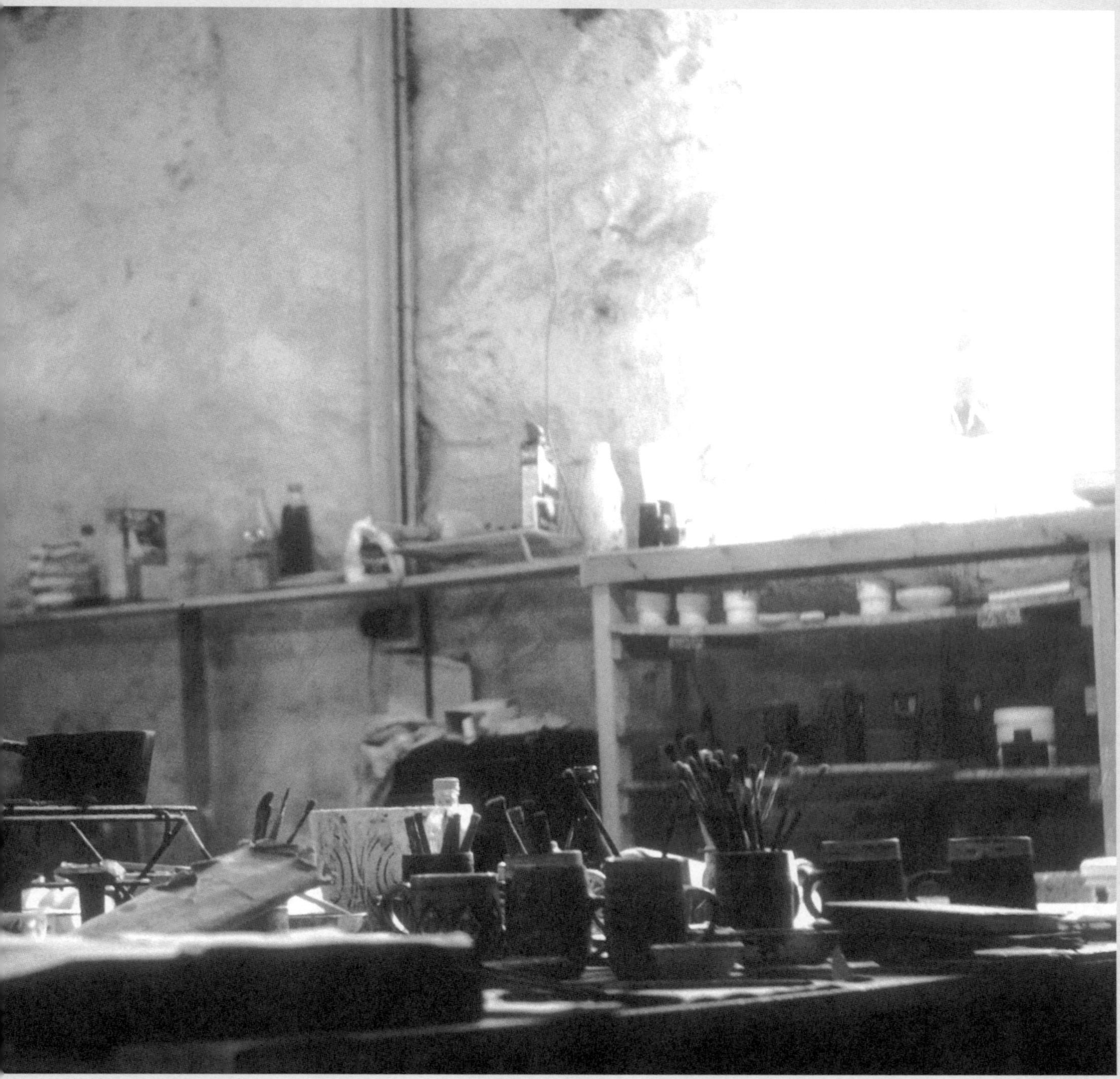

Chapter Two

"You have a good idea, work it out and hope that it is a good idea."

– Stella Benjamin

Soon after taking over the business, the orders which came with the Powell and Wells pottery diminished. Then the buyer from Scotland placed a large order and failed to pay. Benny thinks that he bought so much he had saturated the market and simply could not sell them. This potential commercial disaster acted as a catalyst to Troika, encouraging them to focus their energies on developing their own work. Instead of trying to find new markets for old pieces they decided to produce some new pieces of their own.

Benny had already been using the wheel that had come with the fixtures and fittings of Powell and Wells. He had produced a range of pots in the studio pottery style. These terracotta jugs and vases were quite similar to the other studio pottery in St Ives. They didn't sell in massive quantities but Troika never intended for this type of pot to be a mainstay of the business. Stella says, "Benny didn't want to do the thrown pottery. He did some but he didn't want to throw all day."

With their income dwindling and with little hope of it returning the partners were feeling the pressure and were suddenly aware just how much they had taken on. To add to this pressure Benny remembers how negative local opinion was of their venture,

"The whole art community down in St Ives said to Leslie and I, 'we'll give you three months'. That's what they said." Opinionated, eager to prove themselves and keen to make their own impact upon St Ives and the artistic community, these comments acted as motivation. Bryan, Leslie's brother remembers how,

"It was all slightly daunting; they had no money and didn't really know what they were doing. It was infectious and Leslie and Benny thrived off this nervous energy."

After deciding that throwing was not going to produce enough pots fast enough to support the business, they realised that they already had a way of producing quickly and in large quantities. Powell and Wells had used two small moulds. Troika was astute enough to develop this process. By making this quick economic decision to embrace an industrial process, they would forever separate themselves from the 'arts and crafts' and studio potters in the area.

Leslie had experience of making moulds during his time in London. In order to fund his course at St Martin's he had been employed by one of his former lecturers from Kingston

"It was all slightly daunting; they had no money and didn't really know what they were doing. It was infectious and Leslie and Benny thrived off this nervous energy."

Bryan Illsley

Early experiments with glaze and colour.

Art School to help produce moulds for some prototype rubber shoes. These were complex moulds and often involved many parts. It was obvious to him that as long as they had a basic shape they would be able to make a mould and then cast as many repeats as needed. Immediately he began taking moulds of Benny's thrown pots. Bryan remembers, "Leslie employed what he knew to make it work. He used the technology available."

Leslie had enough experience to embark on the job but true skills and knowledge took a while to emerge. It was difficult to produce large moulds in large numbers. As Kristen recalls, "It wasn't easy. I was there in the beginning when they were trying to make the moulds. Lots of things went wrong. They had lots of trouble with moulds drying. A lot of problems with the slip. It was hard work."

After a few teething problems, the main production process at Troika became slip casting. This involved making a master shape which was then rested in a tray of plaster that covered half of it. After a short period of time the plaster set. The now hard plaster was separated from the master and left half a mould. This process was repeated to produce the other half. These halves were bound together with a bicycle inner tube to form a complete mould. Slip (sodden clay) was poured into this mould which slowly absorbed the water from the

> *"It wasn't easy. I was there in the beginning when they were trying to make the moulds. Lots of things went wrong. They had lots of trouble with moulds drying. A lot of problems with the slip. It was hard work."*
>
> *Kristen Roth*

slip. The slip slowly hardened from outside through to the middle. When the clay reached a desired thickness the remaining slip was poured away for later use. Once the remaining clay had further hardened the mould was removed leaving a hollow shape formed from clay. This process was a revelation for Leslie and Benny and was exactly what they were looking for.

In the evenings, they started making more interesting shapes to use as a master block. They realised that they didn't have to throw but could build a shape out of solid clay. Benny built the 'double base vase', so called due to its distinctive upper and lower sections. These two sections were almost forced together. A curved bowl sat upon a triumphant angular plinth, it looked like there should be flames flickering from the top.

Other hefty forms arrived; a dramatic cuboid column with a tapered top and a large urn. The small kiln would only have been able to hold a few of these per firing, so few were ever made.

Both partners began working with these new shapes. Benny experimented with glazes and texture, Leslie with form. For the observer it makes these early experiments difficult to engage with, they could almost be called conflict pieces where a single identity was yet to establish itself.

They were dark, often black, the design obscured by the dense colour. These pots were radical and tempestuous, they looked like studies of a storm. They were bleak and clouded yet struck through with blasts of inspiration. Like figures in a circus freak show that draw you in with an unpleasant intrigue only to force you back, as if they do not understand themselves and are embarrassed by their existence. The double base vase leans away from you as if retreating into its own shadow. Yet they remain proudly defiant and leave you with an uncomfortable feeling of voyeurism, like you have seen inside a soul laid bare.

The shapes themselves were rarely stable or uniform. Protrusions erupted from the surface, provoking the viewer with almost a violent sexual undercurrent. Pleasure is gained from the severity of the wounds which scar the sides of these shapes. Benny remembers,

"You see all the incision marks I used to dig them in with a knife, hack them... You can see Leslie has been tinkering with it putting nipples on it and all sorts of things... that was the first sort of glaze we ever used, brown, it was a mixture of manganese and cobalt and white glaze, and sometimes when we fired it we would get these bronze streaks because manganese and cobalt at certain temperatures you get a sort of goldy colour. I only found this out by trial and error, nothing to do with the chemistry, there were lots of experiments."

Early 'column' and 'double base vase'.

"We would turn the kiln on, on a Friday night, turn it off on a Saturday. You could sort of time it but it was crucial that it came down at the same point or all the pots would stick together."

Benny Sirota

These objects were effectively being used as testing grounds for new ideas. The pot's large surface areas gave ample room to experiment. Neither of the partners had much experience with firing clay or using glazes and metal oxides to produce colour. They needed to see what would happen inside the kiln: a secretive place where permanent changes occur in the structure of the clay and invisible colours emerge.

In the early sixties firing a kiln was a labour of love as well as science. People could be obsessive. Benny remembers a fellow potter from Pendeen, "Pete Smith. He was good. He fired with coal. He built an old English coal kiln with holes in it. And he used to phone up Culdrose to find out the air pressure because it affected how long his firing would take."

Even for Troika who were using modern production methods it was important that the kiln was on at a steady temperature for a certain amount of time, in order for the pots to come out as expected. Ceramic cones were used to check the progress of a firing. Each cone was designed to melt and bend over after a certain time and temperature had been reached. Someone had to be there to watch when the cone went down and so turn off the kiln. Today kilns are often automatic and controlled by a pyrometer.

Benny said,

"We would turn on the kiln on a Friday night, turn it off on a Saturday. You could sort of time it but it was crucial that it came down at the same point or all the pots would stick together."

It could have been worse. It was not unheard of for a pottery to burn down if a kiln was left on for too long without anyone being present. Also the clay had to be what is termed 'leather dry' before firing, this meant it had a moisture content of less than fifteen percent, any higher and it would explode during the firing. They only learnt this by trial and error.

Troika's experimentation with techniques was bold. Without a paradigm or instruction to adhere to they were creatively fearless. Traditional mistakes cannot be made without a tradition. Troika, however, should not be seen as haphazard. Each experiment was a calculated risk, put through a process of formative evaluation and refined until a piece reached a standard they agreed upon; both in finished quality and visual appeal.

Although inexperienced, each team member had brought intrinsic skills that helped Troika to thrive. Stella and Kristen were both art school graduates and Leslie had his mould making and sculptural background. Benny probably had the most direct experience. He had worked with Daphne Wells but had been around pottery for years. His first wife Wendy ran a pottery in Notting Hill and Benny himself had been employed by Dougie Zadek at Cobham Pottery in 1954. Although only there for a short time this counts as an apprenticeship of sorts. Here he had his introduction to clay, glaze and the kiln, as he explains,

"Dougie was at the Bauhaus, that's where he trained to do ceramics, he was a fantastic thrower, I just used to dig his clay out and mix his clay, weigh it up for him so he had balls of clay. I would also watch how he fired his kiln. That was in the evening because in the day I was working, driving a van for Hennicky's the wine people."

Whilst at Cobham Benny produced a thrown tea-set that he dip glazed, using stencils to achieve a repetitive design. He entered this for the Rural Industries National Pottery Competition and won third prize, coming ahead of all the others at Cobham and many other established potters.

Benny's apprenticeship and own work was carried out in the evenings, alongside a paying job. Leslie too had always worked and had never had the luxury of receiving a full time art education. Troika was motivated by these early experiences and was conceived as a way of facilitating life rather than just simply the production of art.

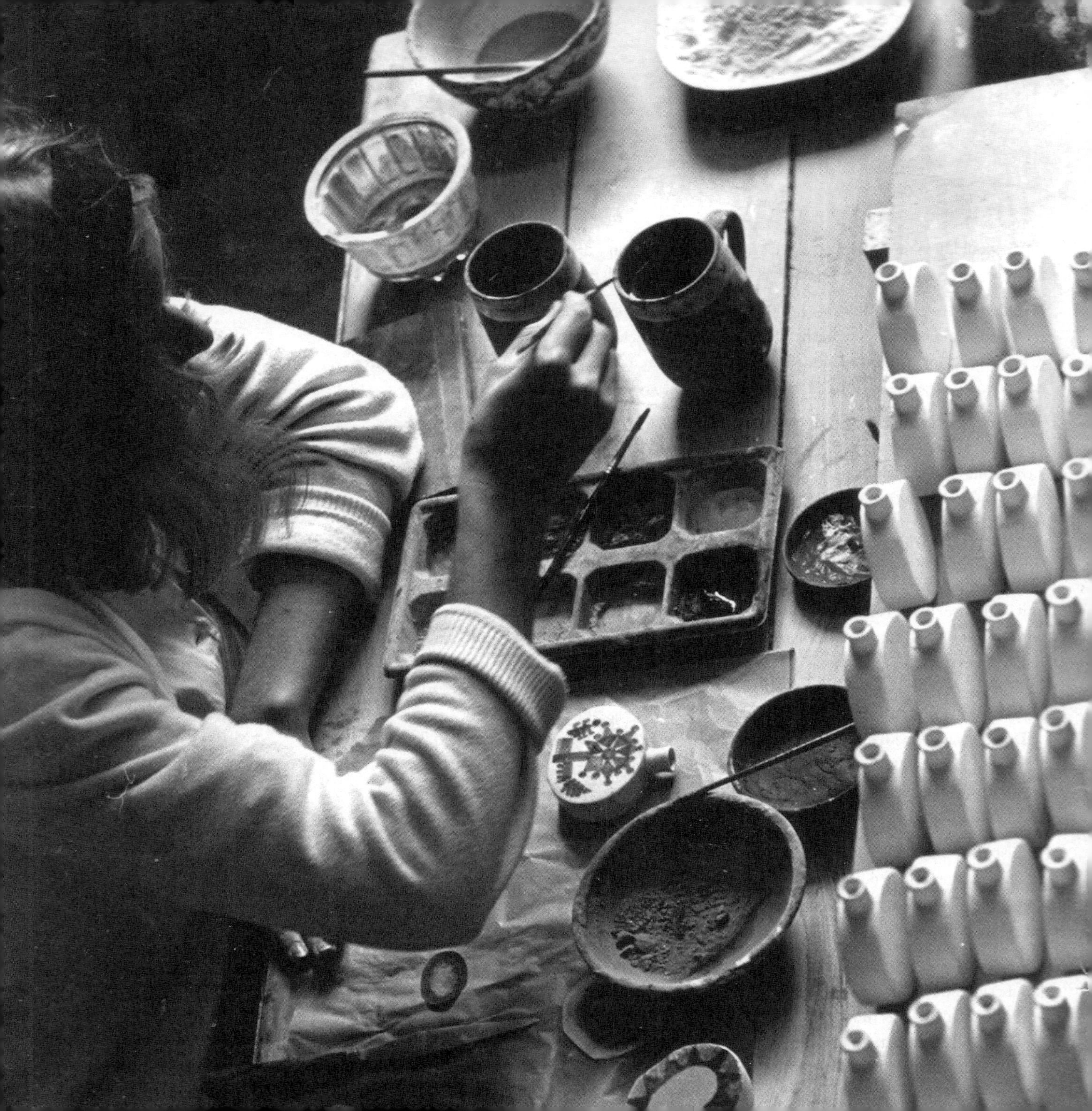

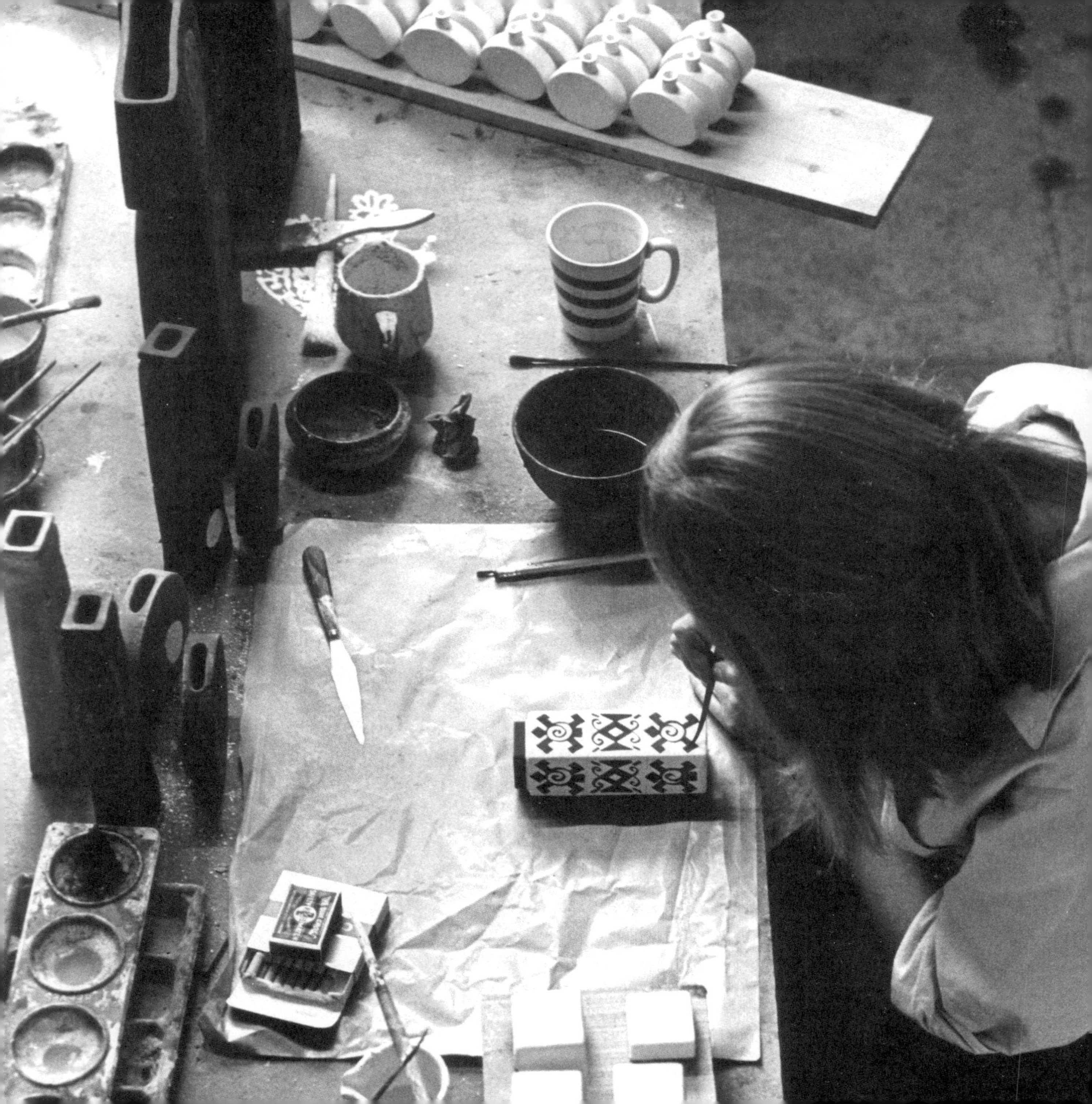

It is also interesting to note that Zadek trained at The Bauhaus, the famous school in Germany that wanted to bring artists together to produce vital and dynamic work for large scale public consumption. It must have been at least an unconscious influence upon the endeavours of these modern young men. It is not too much of a stretch of the imagination to expect Zadek to have spoken of his time there and offered Benny advice, hardly expecting him to start up a project like Troika.

As the experiments conducted at Wheal Dream began to produce consistent and satisfying results, the group worked together to produce a range of stylish modern domestic home-ware that they hoped would be instantly saleable. As well as Benny's shapes, such as the small cylinder, Leslie started to take casts from many different objects in order to produce a master block. Slip casting meant that solid objects could be turned into hollow shapes suitable for use as receptacles. This technique meant that Troika never had to build hollow pieces by arranging flat sheets of clay to form a square shape, which is known as 'slabbing'. Instead, pieces of industrial 2x2 wood became little oblong jars or hollow cubes. The only limits to their casting process were imagination and the size of the kiln.

Troika wanted to create new and interesting work. They didn't want to follow a rule book or become part of a tradition. They set out to create their own unique style and by combining a new attitude with old processes they produced pieces that retained a unique personality.

Traditionally, thrown pottery is round as it is made on a wheel. These little square jars were a quiet revolution, especially in St Ives, where thrown pottery was dominant. A colour palette was also developed for the new range. Benny constantly had to adjust to the challenges of production. Glazes cracked and crazed under firing and colours ran into each other. To maintain control, glazes were kept as simple as possible. There were two glazes, one white, one transparent. For contrast, manganese was added to produce an umber tone. For decoration, patterns were painted in blue over the white glaze or a blue wash was covered with transparent glaze. Cobalt, which gave the blue, was the cheapest of the metal oxides to buy. Stella claimed that the subconscious inspiration for the blue vases came from the local environment,

Previous page
Kristen and Stella decorating.

Below:
Lidded blue 'cuboid' vase, with wax resist flower motif.

"French fishermen used to come in the Sloop. They wore these lovely blue work clothes. The fabric had a light in it because it was fading, it was so tactile. They were smoking Galois, the whole pub smelt of it."

On the oblong vases a lazy flower motif was inscribed within the blue wash. This was achieved by laying a base coat of blue and then painting on wax in the shape of the flower. Once the wax had hardened they dipped the whole piece in a clear glaze. After firing the clear glaze would draw out the colour and make each piece resplendent with vibrant blues and greens that changed as the light fell upon them. The wax would oxidise into carbon dioxide and water and effectively disappear during firing.

Benny also developed the 'chargers' or large decorative plates. Benny threw the original shape and made a design for the surface, coloured using the same blue as the little jars. A complex pattern emerged from an apparent chaos of concentric circles. Some of these patterns were almost arabesque, with continuous streams of leaf-like shapes twisting and winding around each other. The flat circular surfaces were beautiful and show that, from the beginning, Troika was focussed upon style over practicality. These pieces were a direct attempt to attract the public artistically but as they had a flat base they were notoriously difficult to pick up from a surface.

Stella Benjamin was the person who brought the 'chargers' to life on a daily basis. It was her hand that decorated the vast majority of these, continually varying Benny's original designs. Stella had a remarkable ability to create high quality work at high speed.

Stella herself created some of the simple motifs that adorn these early pieces. The most recognisable was the 'scarab' design which was picked out in blue on many of the white glazed pieces. These included the 'oblong lidded jars', 'flasks', 'perfume bottles' and 'trays'.

On the other side of the decorating table Kristen was mainly preoccupied with decorating the 'perfume bottle'. Stella also decorated these popular items and so there was a wild variety in the design upon these pieces. The two decorators were given freedom to paint whatever came to mind. Kristen often used bold colours to paint flowers or suns. Her work shared the aesthetic of the first Troika tiles, inspired by simple, natural imagery.

Investment was needed in order to make this range of new pieces in the quantities required to generate enough income to service their debts. Wheal Dream was only equipped to make small tiles. A new, larger kiln was needed. Stella remembers the purchase of a dough mixer from her Uncle's bakery in Sidcup, Kent. This was needed to mix the clay with water and turn it into slip. Stella recalls, "The mixer was made by Gilbert so we used to call it Gilbert. It was very handy I have to say – make do."

The source of their clay wasn't important to Troika in terms of provenance, only in terms of quality, attributes and price. So they chose to buy a standard semi-porcelain clay from Stoke-on-Trent simply because it was white and was what Powell and Wells used, it seemed to be doing the job.

It wasn't only about making pieces but also about distribution. They needed a van to do deliveries in. Leslie didn't drive so it was down to Benny to source a vehicle. Benny remembers an early stroke of luck,

"This guy came down from Leeds for a long holiday. He was a big pipe manufacturer, he said 'if you want a van I've got a van you can have.' So I went up to Leeds. I've never had such a terrible drive back in my life. It was an old Ford van, quite big but the steering was awful. It lasted a little while but I refused to go very far in it. Luckily all the deliveries were local at the start anyway."

As their new range went into full production they never fully resolved the struggle to produce their ideas with the equipment and procedures immediately available. Early blue jars showed uneven glazing and distorted shapes where the clay had warped when still wet. Colours were never mixed to a chemical formula but by eye. Hot spots in the kiln were learnt and worked with.

Often these small production errors added charm and intrigue to the early work. From these first few months they showcased a stubborn and dedicated commitment to individuality which meant that they overcame problems to produce the objects they wanted to create.

By June of 1963 they had fulfilled their aim of creating a new and dynamic design studio. The new pieces were attracting attention from the local community and from tourists who wandered into their little showroom. A newspaper article in the St Ives Times and Echo confirms how proud they were of their success:

"A team of young craftsmen, working together, have started a design centre – Troika – in Wheal Dream. Basically it is a pottery business, taking over from Powell and Wells but the team plan to expand and include, among other things, ceramics culture and silks screening; to work on interior décor and to hold exhibitions at the centre as well.

"The mixer was made by Gilbert so we used to call it Gilbert. It was very handy I have to say – make do."

Stella Benjamin

"There is an exciting atmosphere at Troika of something new going on 'We hope to experiment with design', said one of the team. 'To use pottery for example not only in the accepted sense of clay vessels, but in new ways, and to adventure with all sorts of other materials as well.'

"...we are tired of hearing how good the Scandinavians are at design' said Jan on behalf of the team 'Its time to help raise British standards'.

"A large dreary looking chamber, once a bakery and once a garage, underneath the seaman's mission has been transformed by the group into a working studio and exhibition room, where visitors can browse and buy and watch craftsmen at their work.

"On display are pots by Sirota and Illsley, ceramic tiles and sculpture by Illsley and an intriguing screen lit up after dark by Mr Brian Illsley, (not for sale)" - **7th June 1963 St Ives Times and Echo "Adventure at Wheal Dream."**

Whilst all the commercial endeavour was continuing at pace there was a small time left over for artistic play. There was always the hope that the new space at Wheal Dream would not only provide a living for them all but would also act as a base where they could develop their artistic aspirations.

In the summer evenings Troika became something much more than a commercial pottery. Bryan's screen would be lit up and their experiments with materials that in the day would be focussed upon developing the business would be freed. Ideas could be explored without being subjected to economic tests.

Their artistic expression was not constrained by a particular form. Leslie and Benny used the space and materials at Troika to produce modern, one-off works of sculpture under their own names. Leslie was familiar with stone and metal but now turned his hand to the materials around him. Pieces were begun in wood, clay or plaster but often were formed from a composite of these materials.

Not only at Troika but many young artists of the day were finding themselves in situations where the old definitions of what materials could constitute art were impractical. Troika's practice could be compared with the Fluxus movement which also emerged in the sixties. Under the leadership of George Maciunas these artists developed the concept of intermedia where different media and disciplines were merged, they challenged the preconceptions of what art could be and what it could be made from.

Although treated with suspicion at the time by institutions built upon old, familiar definitions, it was environments such as the Troika workshop which facilitated the development of art practices. They expanded creation into the forms we are comfortable with today where artists such as Damien Hirst produce work in many different materials. His piece 'A Thousand Years' included materials as diverse as glass, painted MDF, blood, maggots, and water. Tracy Emin has also been at the forefront of promoting the use of fabric in 'high' art, a material once thought as only suitable to produce 'low' art or craft. The debate remains ongoing but familiarity with many different media is often seen as an asset to the modern artist.

Bryan would also spend some evenings, in his own words "mucking around" over at the Troika space developing his own work which included painting as well as sculpture. He remembers,

"At the time Leslie was carving large, colourful shapes out of wood and hardboard. Up to the size of a kitchen table, large zig-zags and other geometrical shapes. He exhibited some of these at the Penwith Gallery alongside Leach and Hepworth. It is likely that the Troika shapes were smaller more intricate versions of these, that these were prototypes for the Troika shapes."

These evening sessions were proving productive. Leslie made a series of reliefs from clay and slip, which Benny fixed with araldite glue onto a board so they could be displayed on a wall. These were sold as Troika and became their first artistic pieces made solely for aesthetic value and without any practical association. Troika exhibited some of these reliefs in 1963 at the Egyptian House on Chapel Street, Penzance. Many pieces were produced especially for this exhibition which may account for the predominance of one-off pieces from this era.

Troika took part in another exhibition which ran from the 30th December 1963 until the 11th January 1964 at the Fore Street Gallery, in St Ives. This was with a collection of Hedda Carrington tapestries. Both of these exhibitions were noted in the local press and were the beginning of Troika's formal entrance into the local artistic community.

Benny and Leslie were keen to develop a line of architectural pieces. Reliefs that were popular at the exhibitions were moulded and mass produced and are known today as Troika 'plaques'. The idea that these could be actually incorporated into the fabric of a building as a focal point, like a mosaic or frieze, must have been the ultimate, if unfulfilled aim. Troika's mass production of their artistic forms also agreed with the aims and practice of Maciunas and the Fluxists who attempted to widen public consumption of their art by mass producing it in order to lower the price, albeit unsuccessfully.

Large relief by Leslie. Shown with a selection of early work.

Troika 'plaques' proved to be very popular. Leslie's 'love plaque' had the feel of a frieze with a narrative story moving across the piece. It was a sardonic take on the progress of a relationship from love to marriage to male subservience, perhaps based upon Leslie's personal experience. Kristen remember a dark undercurrent to the playful energy of the early pottery,

"There were all the marital things. I don't think Leslie was very happy when I was working there. It wasn't a very happy marriage the first one. She wasn't ever about in the pottery."

Another popular design was the flat perspective of the Thames which took inspiration from local artist Alfred Wallis. Both of these designs were somewhat traditional in their subject matter but many of the other 'plaques' were modern and abstract. They seem to represent more clearly the direction in which Troika wished to develop. The most common of these were known as the 'calculator plaque' or the 'stove plaque'. Names not coined by Troika themselves but by collectors in the modern era. Instead of narratives or landscapes they were concoctions of squares and other geometric forms, often coloured with basic shades of white, black and light blue, specifically to highlight the intrinsic shapes.

Chapter Three

"The winters were great it was so empty. I can remember walking along the harbour to work and there being no one around. But in the summer you get bombarded. All the tourists around. It changes so completely."

– Sylvia Valance

The winter of 1963 was coming to St Ives and with it, silent rain-washed streets. Few people would be coming to see an empty grey sea fighting with its own deep torment. Many artists were forced to get other work to see them through the dark months. Before Troika, Benny and Leslie had been doing the same, working odd jobs and getting by. Benny had most recently been a waiter in the 36 Restaurant and didn't really want to go back.

Troika was started as a means to escape this seasonal turmoil and Benny was determined not to be trapped, "I said Les we're not going to become, I don't want this to become a seasonal pottery, 'cause we never made enough money anyway."

As added impetus to gain some financial stability they had mounting debts with mounting interest and rent to pay on Wheal Dream.

They had sold a few pots and reliefs but it was obvious to Benny that simply selling a couple of pots to keen tourists was not going to make the business take off or even pay off what they had borrowed. He thought the only way to break this cycle was to chase the market, to go to where the people always are. He suggested they go to London and seek some buyers,

"It was my decision to break out of St Ives and go for the Heal's contract. I was going to go up on my own but Leslie wanted to come, so we both went. We wrapped the pots in a blanket and went up. Otherwise it would have been just awful, what do you do in the winter? You just make things. We were short of money and we were borrowing. We didn't know it would work we just went up."

So they set off for London. They climbed into the old Ford van and bounced up the A30 with a selection of pots.

The Heal and Son store on Tottenham Court Road seemed the perfect place to start. It represented the best of cutting edge home-ware, designs that would be bought by trendy, up-and-coming young professionals. Those who wanted to dress their homes with a bit of quality. Troika's domestic range was designer and although produced to be affordable, it wasn't cheap. To buy it required some commitment from discerning buyers who were happy to invest in their surroundings.

"I said Les... I don't want this to become a seasonal pottery, 'cause we never made enough money anyway."
Benny Sirota

When they arrived on Tottenham Court Road they pulled up outside the wide façade of Heal's - it was much easier to park in London fifty years ago. The long buildings of that central London thoroughfare loomed down over them as they disappeared inside. The Ceramics Department was on the second floor. Benny tells us what happened,

"We went up and asked the assistant if we could see the buyer. She said 'sorry, have you got an appointment?' So I said 'Oh, we've come up all the way from Cornwall to see you, can you do me one thing'? She said 'What's that?' So I gave her two pots and said 'Just take those in and show him'."

Five minutes later the door was opened and they were beckoned into Mr Ransum's office. He was the principle buyer of ceramics at Heal's. After a quick business chat they were waving goodbye to the helpful sales girl and climbing back in the car with an order for £150 and the hope of more. An impression had been made. This initial order was a lifeline the pottery badly needed. By the Christmas of 1963 three different Troika pieces were featured in the Heal's Christmas catalogue.

Back in St Ives they still needed to generate more revenue. Flushed with their first success, Benny decided to try and generate some more orders for the next summer from local shopkeepers. He travelled all around Cornwall in the little green Ford van establishing contacts and generating sales. Benny was a natural salesman. He was an art connoisseur, he knew what he was looking at and how to convince others of its quality, unlike Leslie who assumed they should know.

Jan had remained a silent partner. He was happy to lend the money and help out from time to time but he had a career as an architect to maintain. Benny and Leslie were happy to grow the business but there was no mythical brotherhood between the pair. Their relationship was more grounded. They were different people of different ages who led separate lives. They had a quiet respect for each other and would discuss every aspect of the pottery before moving forwards. Kristen remembers,

"Benny and Leslie was a very strange relationship, they never seemed to be really pally, they were such different characters, Leslie seemed like a loner in a way. Benny was quite with it... They had their own lives, they weren't inseparable, they were mates and worked together but that was probably enough really. They would meet socially and discussed things, but not all the time."

"We used to go to this theatre in the East End of London. We used to go there a lot. Leslie, Bryan and I went up to the opening of The Establishment in Greek Street, just off Oxford Street, I mean they were Cambridge people but their humour was new."

Benny Sirota

Glazed 'shoulder bottle' with 'gingerbread boy' motif

New shapes continued to emerge; the 'shoulder bottle' was introduced after being cast out of a piece of wood. The neck was offset to one side because Leslie found it amusing. Bottles were supposed to have a central neck. There were very few examples of this shape in its early glazed form. They would have taken up too much room in the kiln to be a dominant feature of production. However, the 'shoulder bottles' exhibited some interesting ideas and led to the introduction of using reliefs in the main Troika range. Leslie was experimenting with casting and there are examples with the 'calculator' and 'stove plaques' either impressed into the surface or placed upon the sides in relief. The 'plaques' were popular so the forms were taken and used on the functional range. This was an attempt to increase sales by tempting the public to buy an appealing design in a practical form. Some of the earliest pieces even feature a small moulded 'gingerbread' boy that doesn't appear anywhere else in Troika's work.

Throughout 1964, the development at Troika continued with the appearance of a new geometric range. The circle was the dominant theme. The cube jars and oblong jars began to feature a bold circle in Manganese glaze set against a white background, the stark contrast in the tones was also explored in reverse. Benny was developing a simple, stylish and confident geometry in contrast to the 1963's washy blues, which continued to be made. He was fascinated by Ben Nicholson, whose work was clearly referenced in these geometric pieces.

Some of Benny's first pieces of Troika decoration featured circles but often obscured or in rows. The circle got bolder until it began to appear as a singular form on a 'plaque' which featured a large yellow, sun-like circle. Suddenly the

Early textured ware

circle was no longer hidden but became an object in its own right; singular and dominant, modern and contemporary.

The circle in the square was a popular design motif in the mid sixties, especially in black and white. This minimalist geometry was very much of the time and these new pieces were soon bought by Heal's, who continued to increase their orders.

This circle meant that glazes were now being used much more efficiently as blocks of dramatic solid colour. The new design was economic both in style and production. It did not require an undercoat of washed colour, a process which was time consuming and difficult to control.

Whilst the geometry was being explored another phase of ideas was emerging. The textured range. This style of Troika was inspired by necessity. Plaster moulds did not last forever, they would start to show noticeable signs of deterioration after twenty pots had been cast from them. Pieces would emerge from the moulds lumpy and pitted where the plaster had worn away unevenly. It was costly and tedious to remake a mould. Leslie was bored and it was starting to feel like work.

Instead of rejecting the pieces, they embraced the deterioration. They began to accentuate the interesting texture and fractured lines with knives or by painting slip mixed with sand onto the shapes. Bryan saw this development occurring,

"Moulds wear out quickly, too quickly to be much fun or be profitable, so they started scratching in designs onto the pots to disguise the flaws of an old mould. From necessity came design."

Leslie working with moulds

> *"Moulds wear out quickly, too quickly to be much fun or be profitable, so they started scratching in designs onto the pots to disguise the flaws of an old mould. From necessity came design."*
>
> Bryan Illsley

The earliest textured pieces were made as kiln fillers and interesting oddities for the showroom. Their total rejection of normal ideas of perfection, such as a smooth finish or distinct lines made them much more exciting to the two partners than the ordinary home-ware that was being sent to Heal's. So they began repeating this process intentionally, enjoying the dynamic result of having a piece of clay that felt alive in their hands. Today these pots seem to touch you back when you handle them.

Benny had been experimenting with colour and found that texturing removed the need to use glazes. They had assumed from the beginning that glazing was essential to the production of ceramics. Since glazes had become limiting they challenged that assumption and discovered a new process as Benny tells us,

"All of the rough stuff was unglazed. That was the experiment, I wanted to fire high so that they didn't rub off and they changed colour slightly. That would take a long time to do if it was painted on a glaze, and it would streak, but on a rough surface you just had to mix the oxides with water and off you go!"

The mass-producing of this idea fully emerged when it was realised that textured clay gave a sharper finish to the decoration. This breakthrough once again allowed Troika to gain more control over the designs. It made firing simple and decoration quicker. The first mass-produced textured pieces were the 'urns', quickly followed by the small 'wheel vases'. The white glaze was still used to waterproof the interior but this just required the pieces to be dipped.

Leslie developed the master blocks for these new textured pieces by pasting sand and slip onto the master block itself. The grade of texturing on a piece was related to the source of the texturing material. In a continuation of their early experiment with materials, slurry from the local mines provided a gentle wave-like texturing whereas sand provided a much more pronounced grain, coarse and rough to the touch. The texture was eventually combined with predominantly glazed pieces to enhance the decoration; we see this through the 'mugs' and the 'small cylinders vases'.

The 'mug' was decorated using the wax resist method. It would first be painted by Stella with a ring of circles and then this design was covered with wax to protect it. Benny would then dip these mugs into a bucket of glaze, wait for the glaze to dry into powder and brush off the excess. He would then fire them in the kiln. When the kiln was opened there remained a half glazed, half textured mug.

Benny, Leslie and Stella were all working long hours to maintain production. Benny was becoming increasingly absent from the pottery on his order runs so the sculptor Peter Ward was occasionally asked to help with casting. Peter lived in St Ives for three years until 1965 and often freelanced for some extra income.

Troika was challenging the local paradigm and creating a distance between itself and other local pottery producers. Troika may have been based in St Ives but forever looked beyond that seaside town for inspiration. Benny and Leslie never lost their ties to London and proceeded to sell most of their work there. They would often use the excuse of delivering their work to soak up a little bit of the blossoming cultural scene and get some contemporary inspiration. Benny remembers,

Early relief, mixed media: Leslie cast a piece of the wall of Wheal Dream to form the basis for a series of real 'wall plaques'. This appealed to his sense of humour.

"We used to go to this theatre in the East End of London. We used to go there a lot. Leslie, Bryan and I went up to the opening of The Establishment in Greek Street, just off Oxford Street, I mean they were Cambridge people but their humour was new."

The early sixties was a time of radical cultural expansion. Theatre, comedy, music and art were all being fundamentally affected by a new generation of excited and educated young people. These people represented every economic background, class and sex. The Education Act of 1944 had made secondary schooling free for all pupils and the school leaving age was raised to fifteen in 1947. The fifties then saw the emergence of 'The Angry Young Men'. A group of mainly working class writers who wanted to challenge traditional English society and its stereotypes. In 1962 the Beatles shot to fame and became new heroes for the working class. John Lennon was a personal hero of Leslie's. The stripping away of tradition, hierarchy and institution was the most significant part of the sixties revolution. Troika was part of these changes and were not only inspired by them but, by their actions, helped make this vision a reality.

Chapter Four

"It's a shame they had to make the 'double egg-cup', but it made them money."

– Kristin Roth

Even with the early success of the showroom and selling to Heal's, Troika was not yet a thriving business with a large profit margin. It was barely providing four people with a working wage. It was likely that they made less than four thousand pounds in the first year as there is no record of a second payment to Daphne Wells, as stipulated in the contract. By early 1965 things were looking bad for the studio, the future was uncertain and they were in danger of losing all they had built.

Heal's were becoming frustrated with Troika as they were not receiving enough pots to keep up with demand. They contacted Troika to ask for more pieces. It wasn't enough to have a market for their work they needed to stay on good terms with their main contractor by being able to give them what they wanted. Although they could barely afford to do so, Troika responded to these requests by borrowing an extra two hundred pounds from Jan to buy a new kiln. One of the small kilns they had bought with the pottery was part-exchanged to get another, larger kiln. This put serious financial strain on the company which was already in debt. Pushed into a corner they had to save money. Kristen was let go. Troika had been an inspiration to her and she left to set up her own pottery, "They had to make me redundant because they could not afford me. I became a waitress and saved up for my own kiln and a wheel and started my own pottery in Porthmeor Studios. It was an old saltings shed." Everyone else now had to work harder to up production and save the business.

Jan was becoming worried about the financial position the business was in. Recently married, he wanted to move away from St Ives to pursue his career. In July 1965 he decided that his time as an investor was over. He had not been creatively involved and could no longer justify supporting Troika by paying the instalments on his loan account. Apart from a small flirtation with wall 'plaques' none of the much-heralded architectural range had emerged. Troika instead had to follow the customers and produce more of what was selling. They came to a quick agreement and split on good terms, with Leslie and Benny taking on his debt, although it seems they had little income with which to furnish it.

A few months after Jan had left, a commercial lifeline was handed to them by Heal's who gave them the contract to produce the 'double egg-cup'. The designer (William) Denis Bishop had placed a patent application in 1963 for an innovative extension to the standard egg-cup. He approached Heal's with the idea and they in turn contacted Troika to see if they could mass produce it. Troika was in an almost unique position on Heal's book of studio potters due to their use of manufacturing techniques. Techniques which would bring down the cost of production and provide larger quantities.

Troika gladly accepted the offer to generate some much needed income. Leslie made a mould from which to slip cast the shape. The use of slip casting caused the neck of the 'double egg-cups' to remain hollow and difficult to clean. They were still battling with production difficulties and the 'double egg-cups' often sloped to one side where the thin wet clay had drooped under its own weight before firing.

The 'double egg-cup' was launched on 9th November 1965 with a national marketing campaign complete with its own flyer and a write-up in the Daily Telegraph. Such coverage was unprecedented for Troika. It was hoped the 'double egg-cup' would encapsulate the mood of post-ration-book Britain. People could now indulge in the small luxury of an extra egg in the morning. The publicity was timed to anticipate the Christmas rush and the 'double egg-cup' went on to sell extremely well. At one guinea each they were not cheap and although Troika would have only received a fraction of this, the 'double egg-cup' kept production afloat and paved the way for more adventurous items. The accompanying saucer could be purchased for an extra fourteen shillings. It was allegedly cast from the lid of a paint can and illustrates the innovative way Troika approached their production process.

Leslie felt a little disappointed to have to rely upon such a 'non-artistic' product which was not strictly designed by Troika. Like everyone else however, he was sensible enough to see its worth. It provided valuable income but perhaps more importantly raised Troika's profile, putting a small studio from the provinces into the minds of the wider public.

The staff were often there well into the evening, using it as almost a second home. Even a washing machine was provided which they used to wash their dust-ridden clothes. These long hours seemed to suit Leslie the most and he began to spend more and more time at the studio.

His wife, Caroline, was at the centre of the St Ives party scene and was attracting all sorts of hangers-on and revellers to their house on Island Road. The kitchen would normally be full of people Leslie had never met, something he was growing less and less comfortable with. He enjoyed painting in the evenings on the kitchen table but now this was becoming less possible. The chaos had begun to force him into the Sloop and then back to Wheal Dream for some peace. Troika was becoming not only a work place for him but a refuge.

'Double egg-cups' commisioned by Heal's, 1965

Benny glazing saucer

The more time that he spent at Troika the more attached to it he felt. He found himself becoming more and more involved in the design process and he started to see Troika as part of his artistic expression rather than simply a way of making money. Stella remembers,

"I thought he was a good painter. He was painting at the start. But he stopped because Troika took over."

With Benny on the road, Leslie was often alone in the studio and gradually began to make design decisions on his own. He began taking the early shapes and literally impressing himself upon them. The relatively undeveloped textured range became Leslie's personal province. Although he kept on renewing the moulds for the profitable home-ware he became more and more obsessed with the potential of the textured line. He began covering the master blocks in clay and affecting it. Not just randomly cutting and stabbing to hide the deteriorating moulds but actually carving free-hand symbols with whatever tools came to hand. Literally he was drawing in the clay.

As Leslie became more involved, so the style of Troika began to change and look to the future as Benny explains,

"Leslie was very much more contemporary of the period than I was, I was thirty, he was twenty... I just used to get a lump of clay and slab it out and say look what about this, that's about right to make a nice thing and I'd leave Leslie to start work on the moulds, which made them more successful."

One of Leslie's great talents was to be able to adapt to the medium that was available and so as his painting became less of an option he focussed his vision upon the pieces he was making at work. He had done this before when he began painting as an alternative to his first love, sculpture. Now he was mixing the two.

Leslie was not an artist for other people but for the personal freedom such a path provided him. Many of his decisions reflected his single-minded personality. Although he sometimes exhibited his own sculpture at the Penwith Gallery alongside The Penwith Society of Arts and his paintings in other local galleries, his works were more often found in places he visited and where he felt comfortable. Bryan, himself now an established artist, saw it as such,

"He exhibited where he saw fit and through the connection he made in the real world. So you were often more likely to find Leslie's work in restaurants and pubs rather than galleries. This shouldn't be used as a reflection of artistic ability though, more as a consequence of his social preferences."

> *"Leslie was very much more contemporary of the period than I was, I was thirty, he was twenty... I just used to get a lump of clay and slab it out and say look what about this, that's about right to make a nice thing and I'd leave Leslie to start work on the moulds, which made them more successful."*
>
> *Benny Sirota*

Leslie's single-mindedness is again demonstrated by the manner in which he left the hurly-burly of the London art world for St Ives. History can be cruel or kind depending on how an action is viewed. But it is apparent that he left London not as a failure but by choice.

When Leslie had completed his course at St Martin's, a close friend, the sculptor Maurice Agis, persuaded him to enter his work into the Young Contemporaries Exhibition of 1960. This was a showcase for the best new artists emerging that year. Two of Leslie's sculptures were chosen by the panel. Other sculptors exhibiting were Menashe Kadishman and David Annesley. The painting category included David Hockney and Peter Phillips. Leslie won the Prix Andre Suisse for the best sculpture as judged by Henry Moore. This was even after some dastardly antics from some of the other exhibitors who moved Leslie's work to the corner of the room in favour of their own. One of the other judges, the surrealist painter and collector Roland Penrose, bought Leslie's prize-winning sculpture. This money, along with the prize, a cheque for £100 funded Leslie's first trip to Cornwall to visit his brother Bryan; the trip on which he was to discover St Ives.

Leslie left London not only marked as a promising young sculptor but with an offer to be Henry Moore's apprentice ringing in his ears. However, Leslie felt that he would forever be in the shadow of the master if he accepted the offer, so he left London for Cornwall to pursue his own vision as his own man.

As Leslie was investing more of his soul into Troika, on the other side of town completely unknown to him, a young woman had made her first visit to St Ives. She couldn't have come closer to Leslie without touching him but the timing wasn't quite right. In July of 1965, Judith Howard had arrived from Manchester. She travelled down with a friend to work the summer season in a local hotel. On her last day she wanted to buy a souvenir for her sister and so purchased two mugs from a shop in Fore Street. She was very taken with them and was told that she could "go down and see them at Wheal Dream for a larger selection". Of course she never went and disappeared back to the north.

Showroom at Wheal Dream, St Ives c. 1965

Chapter Five

"Leslie once said that there was something magical about a square and a circle."

– Penny Broadribb

In the summer of 1966 the whole country was resonating with style and a sense of leading the march of the new world. The Beatles were dominant and England had just won the World Cup. Troika was riding this wave of good feeling and success.

After a difficult first few years, Troika was finally selling in large quantities. The 'double egg-cup' had taken off and Heal's began requesting more pieces with each successive order, sometimes up to £1000 a time. Contracts had also been established at Liberty's in London

Leslie, Benny and Stella could no longer cope. More people were needed at Troika to satisfy the demands of the order book. Benny was now going up to London every other week with the van full to bursting.

They put adverts in the local labour exchange and these were found by Roland Bence and Sylvia Valance. The art world was normally a secretive place where only those with connections or money could enter, so neither could believe that such a job opportunity was up on display. Here was a route into the art world with payment and training. All that was needed was a lot of interest and a willingness to learn.

Roland was employed as a caster and a fettler. Fettling is the process of smoothing down the cast pieces and removing the mould lines and any other casting imperfections, such as air bubbles which would make the lines and shapes on the piece less distinct, especially after repetitive castings. He had come to St Ives with his parents who had bought the Primrose Valley Hotel,

"I think they had ideas of me running it, they had big control issues but I'm afraid I joined the beatniks and Donovan down on the beach and took lots of drugs and things."

When Roland was fifteen he left home and went to work as a cook at the rival Tregenna Castle Hotel. However, he walked out two years later, mid-shift, after a dispute about his contract, which was supposed to include financial help for training at a local college, but that had never happened.

"That was just after lunch, I walked down to the Labour Exchange in St Ives and one of the jobs available was Troika. They had just put in an advert for a trainee and because I had been artistic all my life I was really interested. At about half past two I was having an interview with Benny and Leslie."

Roland's first meeting with the two partners was almost comical. Benny was sat on a stool whilst Leslie stood.

"They played the businessmen, they had to sort of act like they were and they asked me what my interests were. Why pottery? I said I was capable of drawing and stuff but they didn't really want anybody to do that, they wanted somebody to fettle and make all of the things because Leslie was really trying to develop more moulds."

Roland started a couple of days later on five guineas a week. He remembers that when he started they were still making the 'perfume jar', and the 'double egg-cup' was selling well. Leslie had already made a start on a more developed textured range producing about six 'cubes', six 'marmalade pots' and six small 'wheel pots' all of differing designs. He was developing new ideas all the time.

Sylvia was taken on as a decorator at around the same time. She had also left school at fifteen and gone to work in a solicitors.

"I couldn't stand it. It was just by pure chance I found the Troika job in the Labour Exchange. I had no art training whatsoever just did a bit at school but I had an interest. That counted for a lot. There was a lot of work back then; it was easy to walk into work. But not something like Troika, that was something quite different. It wasn't your average sort of job."

As a decorator she started on the slightly lower wage of four pounds and ten shillings a week. After a casual interview Sylvia started painting cracked 'seconds' in order to practice. She remembers finding it a very comfortable environment to be in. The working day wasn't too taxing, it was almost school hours.

"We started at about nine, half an hour for lunch and home at half four. If there was a big order we might stay on. I'd just left school, so to go into a nice small atmosphere like that was absolutely great. You know what it's like when you start a new job of any sorts, let alone one in art, and for someone like me who had no training or anything to do with art. They didn't seem to expect too much… You had a freehand which they liked because you never got two pieces the same."

After a few months Sylvia was painting a couple of shelves of mugs a day. Benny, Leslie and Stella had always prided themselves on the standard of the work they produced. When they took on these two young people, they instilled the importance of quality.

> *"You had a freehand which they liked because you never got two pieces the same."*
>
> *Sylvia Valance*

Leslie with 'double egg-cups'

Roland was impressed,

"That photograph, (Leslie with the 'double egg-cups') that's him for sure that's a good portrait, that's how I remember him. Amazing hands, very creative hands and concentration. That's just an egg-cup but it's not if you can see what I mean, that is a pot and it's not money. It's just something created and that's what he was like. Everything was like that. I can remember now him teaching me how to do it, it was like, serious... but not serious."

Due to their commitment to quality and partly due to a self-taught production process, Troika generated quite a large quantity of seconds, especially when glazing. A piece was instantly rejected if the glaze cracked, known as crazing, if it bubbled or ran, or if there was a fingerprint. Even if the circles were not absolutely perfect a piece would not be displayed in their showroom but instead put outside next to an honesty box.

Roland thinks that Troika began to be successful not only because of the high standards but because it was so different to other potteries that were around at the time,

"St Ives was full of Leach stuff, what I call boring pottery, thrown. People were experimenting with glazes a bit but if you bought a piece of pottery it was a piece of thrown stuff."

Benny and Leslie were working together really well. Leslie was providing a constant stream of new, fresh designs and Benny was finding ways to fire, glaze and market them. The partnership had entered a new phase of stability where each of them had defined themselves a niche and were concentrating upon that. They were constantly in discussion about the future. Sylvia noticed how they naturally complemented each other as characters,

"It never felt like a chaotic approach at any stage. Benny and Leslie were equally involved they seemed to work together really well. They must have had their differences but you wouldn't really notice it. Benny was upbeat too, they seemed to be enjoying it, there was a lot of pride in it."

As his workload outside the studio increased further, Benny began to let the new members of staff take over his former production jobs. Roland was taught to pack the kiln. Sylvia was taught how to mix the glazes and the oxides now that the colours were understood and established. It was still all done by eye, not by measurement, which made it difficult to copy. Sylvia remembers,

"I mixed the blues because I got that nice green colour in there so they insisted I mix it for everybody. That was all done freehand with a teaspoon. Just mixing an oxide powder with water, done by eye. Hence why you don't get two colours the same either. Done when we needed it."

By 1967 production had expanded so much that they bought yet another kiln. This was substantially larger than anything they had used before. They sold the smallest kiln and used the medium-sized one to bisque fire the cast pieces. A bisque firing is when clay is permanently changed into a hard resilient material which makes it easier to glaze. Two firings of the small kiln would fill the large kiln which was used for 'gloss' firing. This is where the glaze is melted onto the piece or the metal oxides set and change colour. The team could glaze and decorate just enough pieces to fire the large kiln once a week. Roland remembers,

"I packed a kiln full of double egg-cups; we used to stack them up one on top of the other, to about five high. The kiln was full of them, about a hundred. We went off to the pub and totally forgot it. Went in the next morning and it was glowing it was literally ready to go poof into flames, I nearly got the sack that day for that one but Leslie stuck up for me and said 'anybody can make that mistake'. When we opened it, it had made the most beautiful sculpture 'cause it had all collapsed a bit and fused together so there were big chunks of this piped sculpture. I don't know whatever happened to it, it was never thrown away it was always admired, it stood on the shelf for ages."

As production increased they had to find somewhere to store all the pieces until they were packed and distributed. It was worse in the winter as they stockpiled for the summer rush. They created space in the already cramped studio but this little stockroom still wasn't enough. The extra pieces began spilling out of the studio and they had to rent a garage across the road.

Demand began to rise beyond their ability to cope. Benny remembers getting a large order for the perfume bottle but they would have found it difficult to produce such a large quantity,

"We could have done it if we had known more about ceramics because all designs could have been transferred but we didn't know."

Although the demand was high for the 'perfume bottle', Roland remembers it was falling out of favour at that time. Troika had a burgeoning sense of identity and the 'perfume bottle' wasn't Troika, it was a relic from Powell and Wells. "There was a manufacturer who wanted thousands of them, there was an order for six thousand of them but they weren't Troika! I thought they were really nice. Stella liked those because she could bump them out. I think it was about how much you could charge for them. They were the smallest pots we made and the prices were pretty low anyway. So they were devaluing the other stuff because people were buying them instead of the Troika. They went about a year after I was there I expect."

The 'perfume bottles' were not the only casualty as they were followed by the slow phasing out of the little blue 'oblong vases'. These were the next cheapest item in the range and were sacrificed in order to raise the average spend.

In 1967 Troika was evolving, Leslie was developing the moulds for the textured pieces and interacting with the clay. Growth did not just mean churning out more and more of the same pieces. It meant development in quality and new designs.

Leslie started to see the potential to create sculpture through Troika. He began work on a concave hemisphere in a square block. It had to have a practical function in order to sell. In the sixties it would have been used as a minimalist ashtray even though there was no groove for the cigarette. Benny claims it could not have been an ashtray as those carried Purchase Tax, whereas bowls didn't.
   "Well he made a square dish. The excise people came round about 'the ashtray'. We told them it was for peanuts."

The circle had already been a feature of Troika's decoration for a long time. The 'ashtray' is important because now the square and the circle have become three dimensional to create the shape of the piece and are not just decoration. This makes the piece sculptural as form was the primary inspiration, not function, which was now up to interpretation. Equally, the glazing was used to accentuate the inherent shapes not just to provide visual interest.

Roland thinks that this was when Troika began to move further away from any association with studio pottery,
   "The square is why they wouldn't accept us as studio potters. I mean when you think about it there wasn't very many people doing square stuff. Nowhere in Stoke-on-Trent was. Occasionally art students would make something but that was hand built slab, one-offs."

"We could have done it if we had known more about ceramics because all designs could have been transferred but we didn't know."
Benny Sirota

The 'ashtray' was made in black too. Cobalt was added to the standard white clay to change its colour. Benny remembers,

"I used to mix them, it was ridiculous we had some white clay and we would mix so much cobalt in it that the clay became black. But cobalt was presumably quite cheap back then, it's not now."

An exciting effect occurred when a transparent glaze was placed on it. A seductive blue glow appeared behind the glaze. These bowls caused great excitement amongst the staff. Then as mysteriously as this effect started, one day something changed, as Roland explains,

"It was the most mysterious thing, it just stopped happening one day. Cobalt has been thinned out for years. Back then, that black clay had a lot of black pigment in it, a lot of cobalt and I think the transparent glaze we were using pulled the cobalt out. That blue was in the clay, when we put transparent glaze in there it somehow pulled the blue out. We contacted the suppliers and they said nothing had changed but we knew that something must have changed."

Perhaps this was a blessing in disguise; it was difficult to continue making these dark objects in such a small studio. A separate mould for the black clay was needed so that the white ones did not have bits of black in them and vice versa. In the end, they had to fire the black clay in separate firings to avoid contamination. Increased demand for the black 'ashtrays' would have caused chaos.

Benny also threw a complementary 'round ashtray' which was then moulded. These weren't as successful as the square ones and so are quite rare today. This was to be one of the last pieces Benny threw for Troika. By now even circular shapes were being cast out of everyday objects. Roland remembers that the large 'cylinders' were cast out of a section of drainpipe.

Troika had made enough of an impact that in 1967, Lucien Myers, a well known and highly reputable critic made the long journey south to visit Troika. He wrote a highly favourable article about their venture which was published by The Studio magazine in their Studio Year-Book of 1967. He noted that,

"Production falls into three main categories. Vases, bowls and dishes – many of which are highly original and fascinating in their shape and decoration. Tableware consists mostly of tea- and coffee-ware and accessory pieces, such as the 'double egg-cup', made specially for Heal's, which has proven to be an outstanding success. Then there are the wall plaques and decorations which are very distinctive in conception and treatment. Decoration consists of

"Well he made a square dish. The excise people came round about 'the ashtray'. We told them it was for peanuts."

Benny Sirota

Troika range, c. 1967

design and patterns being modelled and cut into the clay, sometimes combined with painting, and the use of coloured and textured glazes.

The plaques are essentially modern feeling – as indeed all the pottery produced by Troika – and can give an important accent to a scheme of interior decoration. Several have been acquired for this purpose and built in as permanent features of people's homes."

One inaccuracy of this otherwise well written article is that it named Stella as a third partner. Also, the main photograph accompanying the text is of Leslie and Benny with Bryan, Leslie's brother. This was an old photo and it should not be taken as meaning that Bryan was part of Troika. Although he was often there and was party to many conversations he had no official role in the business. Indeed, in 1966, the year before the article was published, he was offered a job at the Leach Pottery.

Bryan went to the Leach Pottery not as an artist but as a packer, putting the pots in newspaper for transportation. It was a much needed job and he knew nothing about the Leach legend. However, it proved to be a revolutionary experience. He got to have hands-on experience and was amazed by the work. It taught him about intrinsic beauty, how things can be beautiful just in themselves. It solidified his dream of being that solitary artist, creating what he needed to for the sake of creation. It was like the university experience he never had. These highly knowledgeable people, who came to study under Leach the master, taught him a lot about art and opened doors to the St Ives art scene. It was then that he met local artist Breon O'Casey, with whom he would start making jewellery.

All this experience and knowledge came at the cost of distancing himself from his brother, Leslie, who in his dramatic fashion never really forgave him for consorting with 'the enemy'. Bryan remembers,

  "He thought I was joining the hoity-toity set, becoming upper crust, playing their silly game and Leslie hated the brownness, the treacly running glazes, like syrup over a sponge pudding he would say."

"We used to go to the Leach Christmas party. A lot of the potters were invited up there to have drinks and food... I didn't appreciate it then, when you're seventeen you don't. You are not aware of the significance of everyone in the same room."

Honor Curtis

Roland recalls that there was always a friendly rivalry between the two, now established businesses. The two studios occupied different ends of the same small town but no-one took the competition as seriously as Leslie who appeared vehemently opposed to everything that went on at the Leach pottery.

"At one point we nearly had a Leach team and a Troika team for five-a-side football... Those days were great in St Ives. It was really good. We occasionally used to go up and pack the Leach kiln because that was a big event. Now and again we would help out Hepworth, shift some of her sculptures through the streets. I used to do that sort of thing too. So there was a gang of us, but we were outside of the St Ives artists we were never accepted. And I'm not sure if that was Leslie's attitude rather than theirs. He took a real resentment towards it."

Opposite:
Round 'ashtray' –
Featured piece moulded from
original thrown by Benny Sirota.
Decorated by Sylvia Valance

Above:
Square 'ashtrays' –
Designed by Leslie Illsley.
Left: Glazed by Benny Sirota
Right: Glazed by Honor Curtis

Chapter Six

"We were oblivious, we were in our own little world. The only contact we had with the other artists was when we went up to the Leach at Christmas. No potters or artists came up to Troika just actors and playwrights."

– Sylvia Valance

In 1967 the oil tanker Torrey Canyon took an unsolicited short cut through the perilous waters around Lands End and struck Pollard's Rock on 'The Seven Stones Reef'. Oil flowed out of its shattered hull and even reached the beaches of St Ives.

Alongside this environmental crisis, relationships at Troika were also on the rocks. These events had their roots in the early sixties. Both Leslie and Benny had been liberally enjoying the fruits of a bohemian St Ives. Between them they experienced everything from heartfelt promises to elope, to awkward confrontations with the local families. As young men they emerged unscathed but they were now older and things were becoming serious. For them, 'free love' was coming to an end.

Until 1966 Benny and Stella had been living in a house on Seaview Terrace, near to Wheal Dream. They left because they had bought Giew House, a lovely cottage in Cripplesease, a few miles out of town. However, in the autumn of 1967 living and working together took its toll upon Benny and Stella. Benny had to leave.

Stella still came to work and would arrive at 9am to start decorating. Benny stayed away until 5pm when she had gone home. A sensible choice perhaps but one that was awkward for everyone. Stella eventually made the decision to leave Troika, "That's how it worked for a while but I thought I can't do this."

In very similar circumstances, Leslie was experiencing relationship problems. He had just bought a house, 6 Bowling Green, in St Ives with his wife. For the past few years Leslie's relationship with Caroline had been affected by his growing commitment to Troika and his disillusionment with a chaotic home life. Despite his daughter Saskia growing up fast, he was spending more and more time at the studio and was hiding his growing inner turmoil through work and drink. Something had to give and by the middle of 1966 Leslie moved into 3 Seaview Terrace which had been recently vacated by Benny and Stella. The house was owned by Barbara Davies who was also the Secretary to The Penwith Society.

To add to the confusion, Leslie had recently met Judith Howard, the same young woman from Manchester who had bought some Troika for her sister the previous summer. Judith had returned to St Ives and become a regular on the party scene. The two of them spent a couple of weeks getting to know each other before winter came and Judith had to go back to Manchester again.

Caroline meanwhile decided that she didn't want to stay in the house she had bought with Leslie and disappeared with Saskia. Leslie took Judith up to see the house and an unsightly mess greeted them. Judith remembers,

"All the beds were upside down. It was really ghostly. This empty house that had been vandalised, newspaper strewn everywhere. Leslie was in tears." He decided that he had to claim back his home and moved back in.

Leslie, having split from his wife and daughter, passed what otherwise would have been a lonely winter in the company of Barbara and by the time spring came round again she was pregnant. With one child away with her mother and another on the way he couldn't cope any more.

Confused, Leslie ran away to London to see his parents. His mother was pleased to see him but he was told in no uncertain terms by his father that 'he had made his own bed and could bloody well lie in it'.

Leslie's relationship with his father had been tense since childhood. George was by some accounts a drinking man with an outdated chauvinistic attitude to life that included dominance in the home. He saw himself as a king in his castle of working class struggle. He had a plan for his sons that amounted to little more than them getting a 'real job' and paying their way. As soon as they were old enough to make their own decisions, Leslie and Bryan decided to reject their natural place in his scheme by choosing art. George never forgave them. Leslie returned to St Ives in a worse state than when he had left and was never to return to his childhood home again.

Judith returned to St Ives and found Leslie in the midst of chaos. John Davies, Barbara's child, was born in July 1967. Leslie allegedly went and visited Barbara and the new baby. It didn't go well. Barbara moved away from St Ives and Leslie never contacted them again for reasons that will forever remain with him.

In the autumn, after gaining repeated assurances of future fidelity, Judith moved into 6 Bowling Green with Leslie. Benny was already sleeping on the living room floor having just broken-up with Stella. Judith changed Leslie a lot. Kristen puts it well, "Lovely Leslie, he did like the girls didn't he." But now he was a bit older and hopefully after recent events a bit wiser. He had found Judith, someone like-minded whom he felt strongly about. Judith recalls,

"You could see how people would be annoyed. People would say 'oh he's got himself some young chick', that was me! I looked after him. As a child Leslie had been neglected. I was neglected too. I left Manchester, did my Dick Whittington thing because I had no home to go back to. Leslie was very attractive, to men and women, but he always used to say they only want me for sex. So we formed a deeper relationship. Leslie liked Barbara but she wasn't someone who he could settle down with. She offered him a place to stay; she saved his life in a way. Leslie just walked out on Caroline."

Troika had begun with the feel of a family business. Benny had been in a relationship with Stella; Bryan Illsley had been around offering ideas and support. By the end of 1967 the original team were no more. Stella left and with her went the fabulous decorating on the 'chargers' and 'D-plates'. She remained friends with Leslie and Judith after her departure. Judith often went to see her on a Saturday for lunch-time wine, "We would soon be down the shop for more. It was a crazy life really. But that was what we were after."

Stella kept a close alliance with the Illsley brothers. Out of work she went to see if Bryan could give her a job. Bryan was now working with Breon O'Casey, a highly regarded painter who had turned to jewellery to make some money. They became life-long friends and colleagues,

"I asked Bryan Illsley, 'give us a job', because I've always been able to use tools. I did a bit of sculpture when I went to Regent Polytechnic. I'd worked for Dennis Mitchell. I was on a month's probation with Bryan and Breon but I was there for 13 years, so I must have passed. I became a jeweller. I just had to earn a living."

It wasn't unusual for notable artists in St Ives to produce more commercial items to pay the bills; this was one of the original motivations that had started Troika. St Ives was developing a real arts industry; there were jobs to be had, especially at Troika. Now, four years on, a whole group of people were working there. Marilyn "Murphy" Pascoe joined the expanding workforce in mid 1967. Honor Curtis was brought in to replace Stella in October 1967.

Honor had previously worked at the local Woolworths. She asked for the day off to get her hair done for her boyfriend's 21st birthday. Her bosses refused but she took the day off anyway. When she returned to work she was sacked. Immediately after this potential crisis she remembers, "I heard about this job at Troika and literally ran down there..."

Honor had been inspired by art as a teenager and recalls,

"My art teacher and my head teacher had written to my parents saying you should really let her go to Art College. But I had to leave school at 15 because I was 1 of 5 children. I really

"It took a long time to train... drawing the circle and painting it by hand, you had to get that circle perfectly before they would let you decorate any pots."

Honor Curtis

Stella decorating in the studio at Wheal Dream

wanted to go to Art College but there was just no possibility of it. So to get a job at Troika was amazing."

For many parents of that era, art was not a valid career choice. Art school was seen as a way of avoiding 'real' work with little hope of making an income at the end.

Benny remembers playing snooker with her Dad, "When he found out that she was going to work for Troika, he came up to me and said 'my bloody daughter is not going to work for you', he was furious; he thought we were all rapists. He was OK though, I got to know him, but he was terrified that his girl could be working for us."

It wasn't only Honor's parents who had their doubts. The beatniks had gone but only in name, their successors were the hippies. They would hang around outside of the Sloop on 'Dobbles wall'. Even as late as 1967 St Ives still had not gotten used to its new inhabitants, some of whom were artists. Honor remembers,

"They would all lie on top with their guitars and they were fascinating, all with long hair. This is probably why my mother didn't want me to go to art school because she thought I was going to turn out a hippy... it was a very religious town you see and a lot of people didn't like it, there was a big division, the art people and the local people and really not many crossed over"

Roland agrees,

"I remember there used to be a bandstand opposite where the arcade is now, a big metal grid hanging out over the sea and everyone used to congregate on there. That was kind of the art students. Donovan was living in a pill box, sleeping rough, myself and a couple of others used to take a bottle of cider down there and smoke spliffs and drink and stuff. One of the St Ives fishermen picked Donovan up from the band stand and threw him in the sea. That was quite amusing."

At Troika, Leslie and Benny were looking for people with the ability to learn new skills but who also had what they considered to be the right attitude to work. There are striking similarities in the stories that Honor, Roland and Sylvia tell. They all talk about Troika as an opportunity, almost a blessing. It offered a way of escaping the drudgery of work by replacing it with a purpose and a pride. Honor agrees,

"It was Leslie who interviewed me. I was a bit cheeky at 17. He said to me, 'are you local?' 'Course I am, I live here don't I?' and that's why he said he gave me the job. Right attitude I think."

Sylvia thinks that the atmosphere they created at Troika came directly from their own life experience,

"None of us were over the top we all came from quite ordinary backgrounds, there was nothing pretentious about them (Leslie and Benny). They treated everyone really well... Actually they did offer to teach me to throw pots, I actually refused! I think 'why did I do that, why did I refuse?' They would have trained me during working hours, so they were definitely encouraging."

Both partners knew what it felt like to have to fight for artistic opportunities. Benny left Manchester Art School at 14 having qualified in art but was given no encouragement to pursue it. When he went for his interview for National Service, the Army Officer who interviewed him thought he was only qualified to 'clean the latrines' simply because he had qualified in art. He never served though, due to a heart murmur. His real education occurred in Earl's Court in the fifties.

When he was eighteen, Leslie's talent was noticed by his sculpture tutor at Kingston Art School where he attended evening classes. Unfortunately, Leslie too had to go off to do his National Service in Cyprus. He continued sculpting whilst he was there. This was soon noted by his Commanding Officer who allowed Leslie to skip duties in order to sculpt him a water feature and assorted garden ornaments.

It was at Kingston that Leslie and his brother Bryan had an epiphany. They borrowed books from the library on Cezanne and Van Gogh and suddenly realised that you didn't need to be royalty to be an artist. As Bryan says it gave them a working model for art. In reality, both Cezanne and Van Gogh were backed by their relatives so hardly provided a true working model. Leslie rather mythologised their experience and made them heroes. However, it was these artist heroes that inspired Leslie to live his dreams. With Benny, Leslie went on to live his own working model for art which in turn provided opportunity for other young people to enter that world.

Anyone who came to work at Troika had to serve an apprenticeship in order to practice and become comfortable with the decorative techniques. Stencils had been abandoned long ago in favour of an individual hand and eye which would help to keep the pots unique. Honor remembers, "It took a long time to train... Drawing the circle and painting it by hand, you had to get that circle perfectly before they would let you decorate any pots."

Honor became part of a natural system whereby experienced decorators would actively teach the newcomers. This started with Stella teaching Sylvia, who then taught Honor. Anne Lewis arrived in 1968 to take the number of decorators to four. Honor would then have the honour of teaching Anne and so it continued. Honor remembers Sylvia as "a brilliant decorator, everything was very precise; everything was very clean and neat."

It was more interesting for the decorators to work on the pieces which Leslie hadn't already carved into. Pieces like the cylinders. Here they had more artistic licence rather than just applying a wash or picking out bits of design already there. They were given the freedom to create their own patterns, as long as they were geometric, not naturalistic.

Honor remembers, "You had to mark out the design in with a pencil... When I had been there about a year I asked Benny and Leslie if I could try something a bit different, so they said 'carry on.' So I started using different band widths, just to make it a little more interesting because it was boring sometimes. The worst to do would be the tall cylindrical ones. Because of their very height they were never straight, so when they were going round you had to be moving with them. When they went into the kiln and they were slightly wet they would tilt..."

Benny remembers that they never interfered with the decorators' work. All that was required was that the order book was filled. If a certain type of design or colour was requested by a shop then Troika would obviously respond. If there was no direct request the decorators would change the design as they got bored. Benny said,
 "The only stipulation was if we needed more fawn pots then they had to do more fawn pots. I don't think anyone did any two pots the same. You are limited to how many oxides you can use so there is bound to be a crossover but they stayed there because they were free to do what they liked."

Working at Troika was not an easy job but it was fulfilling. The decorators were treated as individuals and expected to make individual work. Each piece started as a limited run from the mould and then became unique through the hand of the decorators as Sylvia explains,
 "There were all sorts of shapes. Each piece was individual really, each one was hand decorated and Leslie was always changing the moulds. There were all sorts coming out when I was there."

The idea of individuality within the collective was embodied physically by the introduction of the monogram, the decorator's initials which appear on the bottom of nearly every piece of

"It was Leslie who interviewed me. I was a bit cheeky at seventeen. He said to me, 'are you local?' 'Course I am, I live here don't I?' and that's why he said he gave me the job. Right attitude I think."

Honor Curtis

Troika from 1966. The monograms allowed each of the young decorators to take ownership of their work. Sylvia felt like their input was valid and recognised,

"There was a pride in the work, you felt that you had done your best for them and they genuinely appreciated it. It wasn't just do as you are told, you were allowed to put your own stamp on things, literally. You were treated as an individual and kept as an individual no matter how many people were working there. It was just so different to work there, it was great. I can never remember them being short tempered or shouting at anyone."

As with much at Troika this practice had its roots in pragmatism. Now that there was more than one decorator it was useful to know who was responsible for each piece. Either to praise them for particularly good work or to keep track of any drop in standard or motivation. The monograms have now become a defining feature of Troika. They allow collectors to recognise and appreciate each decorator's unique hand, as well as helping to date the pieces. As Stella or Kristen were never asked to sign their work, this practice started with Sylvia, who remembers,

"I wrote the S over the V or the other way round I can't remember. We never used to hand sign any of the smaller stuff, the 'mugs', 'marmalade pots' it was usually the bigger pieces that got hand signed. I was told to do that from the start."

It is worth stating that the monogram does not credit a designer but a decorator. Leslie rarely, if ever, signed a piece of Troika because he very rarely decorated any with oxides or glaze. He only ever carved or modelled the master block. Even outside of Troika he rarely signed his paintings. Quite arrogantly he felt that people should automatically know his work. There is a mark that is likely to be him but could possibly be a clever modification of the trident symbol when Jan left. One prong is missing now there were only two partners.

Benny only signed the bottom of a piece when he had dipped it in glaze, not when he had finished a design. There is no correlation between the appearance of a mark on the base and the origins of the design, as has been suggested.

This is where Troika distances itself from ordinary industrial practice. A factory-made piece will inevitably have been created by a long list of people, all of whom contribute different skills to its creation. In the hierarchy of skills it is often the designer whose monogram will appear on the bottom of the finished piece alongside the factory mark. This occurred at Sèvres, the large French ceramics manufacturer, for example. However, Troika did not subscribe to this hierarchy.

The earliest pieces do not have any writing on the base but are marked with a trident. Where the trident symbol is embossed it was carved into the mould. When they started selling in large quantities a rubber stamp was used for speed and efficiency. It was still in use when Sylvia started but soon after, the decorators were encouraged to write 'Troika St Ives' on the bottom instead.

Early embossed trident symbol

Chapter Seven

*"Leslie made non-practical, radical art objects.
He hated most of what other people were doing,
he was angry. He wanted to be radical, not a
city-cursing provincial either, he wanted to be
in the mix. Not serve a clique."*

– Bryan Illsley

By 1968 Troika was an established business and had become well known in St Ives. Not only that but Troika had spread its influence away from the peninsula and into the world. Exhibitions at The British Week in Stockholm, organised between Heal's and Swedish department store AB Nordiska Kompaniet led to sales in Scandinavia.

Benny remembers, "I went to a place in Baker Street which sold to overseas buyers only and that's when we started selling overseas. From that we got America, Bloomingdales, which was about £1000, and Sydney, Australia and more in Sweden. There were no repeat orders unfortunately."

The most important events at Troika in 1968 have their roots two years earlier when Benny and Leslie were in the midst of personal crisis. In September 1966 they both had pieces of sculpture in the Penwith Society Autumn Exhibition. Leslie exhibited a piece called "Duo" and Benny a piece called "Circle in Space." They shared the gallery with Barbara Hepworth and Dennis Mitchell. Bernard Leach exhibited in the pottery class. Leslie also had the pieces "Riff" and "Duo" in the subsequent Associate Members show in October, 1966. However, this was to be the last time they would exhibit independent work.

Not long after Bryan went to work for Bernard Leach, Leslie had rejected the artistic community of St Ives and decided to go it alone. He began expending all of his artistic energies upon Troika. This change in attitude was facilitated by an offer from Heal's in 1967. They asked Troika to put on an exhibition of their new contemporary lines. It was a chance for them to showcase their most outlandish designs. As with the very early exhibitions at the Egyptian House and the Fore Street Gallery, Leslie saw this exhibition as a way to create pure art objects.

Here was an opportunity to be able to create work simply for the pleasure of expression. Purely for aesthetics without any practical caveat tacked on at the last minute to make a sale. Behind his front of cynicism he was aching for an opportunity to be recognised by the art world. He had shunned the world of the galleries and here was the opportunity to establish Troika's sculptural heritage. Leslie decided to make a series of pieces which Benny called "Sculptures for Living". He obsessed over the designs for months. Honor remembers, "He was a man of few words Leslie, very focused on what he was doing. He had a real instinct for what he was doing, I mean to come up with the concept was way ahead of its time."

Leslie had to leave the studio to have enough room to make the moulds for these new pieces. He found a derelict house on Back Road West. It was a few doors from Alfred Wallis' house, the famous fisherman turned painter. Judith remembers,

"When I met Leslie he was just about making the moulds for the Heal's exhibition. The pottery in St Ives was too small for him to be making these moulds, so they found this derelict cottage on Back Road West, near the Penwith Gallery. The pottery managed to rent one of these cheaply and so Leslie was ensconced in his little cell making all these moulds, away from the pottery. It was like a beach, there was plaster and moulds everywhere."

Although he enjoyed the creativity he found the house very lonely and ached to be back amongst the hurly-burly of the Troika workshop. Leslie didn't like working by himself. When Leslie emerged from his hibernation and brought the pieces for the exhibition to Wheal Dream, Roland was impressed,

"I remember him bringing them in before they went up and I remember being pretty stunned at how different they were. I really liked them."

Leslie had fashioned an innovative set of geometric sculpture out of clay. Interlinking moulded elements combined to create complex forms, unusual in a substance like clay. The shapes included towers of circles, blocks spliced together along diagonal lines and spheres floating on corrugated plateaus. The moulds from the larger square dishes were inverted to create what came to be affectionately known as 'Bridget Bardot's Bottom' which explicitly illustrates how the 'ashtrays' were the antecedents of these sculptural pieces, as Roland explains,

"I think Leslie had the big ones in mind already. You can see the 'ashtrays' in it. This was really clever, they were made so the shapes would interlink. So you could take different shapes and stick them together in different ways. You had five different moulds which you could make thirty different shapes out of. To get something square and do that was unique."

All of the angular shapes were enhanced by a sparse modern tonal palette of white, black and red. Many pieces were dip glazed by Benny in classic white. Others were painted black or red. Some shapes were cast out of the standard white clay and others of the remaining black, cobalt clay which had made the earlier black 'ashtrays'. Some pieces were made out of black and white shapes stuck together. Leslie connected some of the separate sections together internally, leaving an external gap which made the two sections visibly separate

"Perhaps Leslie didn't have the temperament to be an artist in the classic sense. He didn't like working on his own he liked the group and he loved being amongst his staff at the pottery. He couldn't work for years on something no one cared about just because he had to, he needed an audience."

Bryan Illsley

Leslie working in St Ives

"Sculptures for Living" wall reliefs

yet coherently bonded. A neat piece of innovation which would become a feature of Troika's sculpture. Roland remembers,

"He stuck black pieces to white pieces and what do you use to stick black to white? That became interesting, that developed the gap. Which is what I really like. I like the idea of it being stuck together but you don't know how it's done."

With the promise of an exhibition Leslie produced many fine pieces of sculpture. They have a striking architectural quality and were an attempt to step away from domestic production. Most of these pieces had no function; tall objects that could have been vases often had holes in both ends to make them redundant of purpose.

There was an obvious concern that non-practical pieces would be difficult to market so they often focussed on potential function when describing them in publicity. To this end one new shape, the tower of cylinders, was converted into a lamp. This attempt at marketing the work shouldn't detract from the original intention. The exhibition was intended to produce 'Sculptures for Living.' Sculpture for people to live with whilst at the same time sculpture which generated an income for those who made it.

Each piece was a self-contained unit that seemed to harbour a grand vision. A vision that would dominate the landscape if scaled up to the size normally associated with bronze. According to Benny it was always Troika's dream to be able to make grand large-scale sculpture but they continued working with the assets they had and produced something unique through that process,

"We had visions of doing great big sculptural, ceramic things on walls; you know which Barbara Hepworth was doing in metal and stuff."

These exhibition pieces did not dominate as a larger-scale item might. There was no need to go outside and stand there in awe cowering beneath their mass. Each piece could be appreciated as a whole, as if momentarily the viewer became a giant and was appreciating the scale of the world around them in miniature.

Partly due to financial and practical concerns Troika were forced to limit their vision to the size of their kiln. This was the limitation at the heart of Troika's appeal, it allowed the buying public to connect with the pieces. Troika didn't need a grand building, museum, gallery or garden to give their pieces proportionality.

In February 1968 Benny and Leslie filled the back of their recently purchased Mini van with these new shapes. They put the van on the night train to London and went to find their sleeping compartments. Judith had come along for the adventure and the three of them drank the bottle of whiskey Leslie had brought with him to celebrate.

Once in Tottenham Court Road they spent a whole day setting up the exhibition. The sales staff tried to put dried twigs in the shapes which frustrated Leslie as they were altering the sculptural lines. He ran round trying to remove them but one still remains in the photos.

After a long day, finally the space was set and they all went to celebrate a job well done at a Greek restaurant. Later they

"Sculptures for Living" exhibition, second floor, Heals and Son, Tottenham Court, London

"We had visions of doing great big sculptural, ceramic things on walls, you know which Barbara Hepworth was doing in metal and stuff."

Benny Sirota

Poster for the Austin Reed Gallery, including 'Troika Group'

went back to a London flat owned by a friend from St Ives. Benny left after a few days and drove back to Cornwall. Leslie and Judith stayed on to see the sights of the city, returning a few days later on the train. Benny remembers that, "We took over the whole floor and sold about a third."

He admitted that this was not as much as they had expected to sell. Something had gone wrong. They were full of hope for these new pieces, because it was felt that they had artistic merit. They even fitted in with the Zeitgeist. Magazines were showing pictures of new clean-living, white houses with white interiors. The Beatles were driving around in a white limousine and were about to release The White Album in November. Designed by artist Richard Hamilton, it was seen as the high water mark of sixties minimalism. Leslie bought one of the numbered copies on the first day of its release. Roland agrees that Leslie would have found it ironic that when he pulled the record out of the sleeve it looked remarkably similar to a Troika 'ashtray', a black circle in a white square.

The St Ives Group
painting sculpture & ceramics

The answer to what went wrong is perhaps more prosaic. If the pieces were in the right time, they were in the wrong place. A shop is not an art gallery. These new sculptural pieces were an extravagance for anyone looking to buy a functional item. They were complicated to make and priced accordingly. Perhaps they would not have been expensive for a wealthy collector of traditional sculpture but they definitely were for regular purchasers of Troika.

In this exhibition year Troika also had another show in London. It was in the Austin Reed Gallery on Regent Street. Benny remembers,
  "We were in an exhibition representing St Ives art, Barbara Hepworth and everyone exhibited there. A lot of the old Heal's pieces went in. A lot of reliefs. In fact a lot of artistic pieces went to that exhibition."

Here, perhaps unsurprisingly, they sold. In an art gallery, alongside the best St Ives had to offer, Troika claimed its place at the high table.

"We were in an exhibition representing St Ives art, Barbara Hepworth and everyone exhibited there..."

Benny Sirota

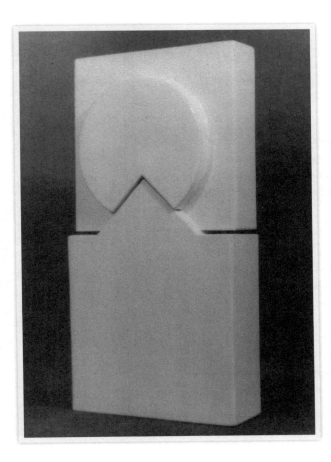

"Sculptures for Living"

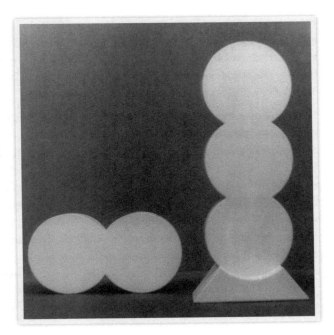

There is an important point to raise here, which lies in the detail. On the poster Troika was listed as 'The Troika Group'. Even when they spoke about Troika or wrote its name on a letter-heading they simply called it 'Troika'. The sign on Wheal Dream said 'Troika'. Never 'Troika Pottery'. The only place where it was referred to as a pottery was on Heal's marketing material.

The partners didn't see Troika as a pottery. That word had overtones of craft and domesticity which felt suffocating. Whilst they had a commercial side which produced domestic ware, their vision extended further than that. "Sculptures for Living" fulfilled their potential.

It is more authentic to consider Troika as being a group of artists who produced quality work. Part of which was art, another part craft, another part utilitarian. With some pieces of Troika it can be difficult to draw a distinction between the three, which only seems to raise the question whether such a distinction is useful or even necessary?

The philosopher David Novitz has argued that where there are classificatory "Disputes about Art" they are mainly inspired by societal values of what art is allowed to be rather than a theory of aesthetics of what art actually is. (Novitz, David, "Disputes about Art" Journal of Aesthetics and Art Criticism 54:2, Spring 1996). Arthur Danto in his essay "The Artworld" (Journal of Philosophy, 1964) also suggests that cultural context and institutions convey the definitions of what art can be. Many progressive, modern representations of art have been subject to such critical dismissal. Examples of this include the original critical rejection of Impressionism, to the popular disdain shown to each year's Turner Prize finalists by the tabloid media.

In Troika's case, the predominant issue regarding the judgement of whether it is art or not is their use of clay. A material traditionally considered to be craft or 'low' art and thus not deserving of a place in a gallery. This is why they so disliked calling their studio a pottery. But in the end it is not the material but what is done with it that counts. Edmund De Waal tells us in his book "Twentieth Century Ceramics" (De Waal, Edmund, Twentieth Century Ceramics, Thames and Hudson, London, 2003) that the German expressionists Ernst Barlach and Paul Rudolph Hennig had already argued that sculptors had become 'blind to clay' and its potential. De Waal also quotes Paul Gauguin who had asserted that "ceramics was a 'central art' not just a decorative appendage to other greater arts, and offered a different way of pursuing sculpture". Despite this, Troika was rejected by many local artists such as Roger Hilton and Karl Weschke, specifically for their use of clay.

Even Troika's process is directly comparable to traditional sculpture, where casting is widespread. It could be thought ironic that where sculptors would destroy their original clay model during the bronze casting process, Troika instead created a permanent piece of sculpture in clay from a plaster mould. Although Leslie would have loved the opportunity to work in bronze the Troika pieces were never supposed to be replaced with bronze, they were made in clay. The material should not detract from the artistic intention.

Troika's work could be thought to be much more pertinent today where the spectrum of art appreciation in Britain is much broader. The definitions of what constitutes art are much freer and rely more upon what the piece is trying to tell us than how it was made or what it was made of. To this extent, galleries now exhibit artworks made from many materials that were previously considered only suitable for craft purposes, such as plastic or indeed clay. Galleries also promote examples of artistic practice such as photography which, like casting, allows reproduction. Art is no longer solely the promotion of a singular object which can be hoarded by the collector.

Alongside the removal of many socio-economic boundaries, the twentieth century witnessed the opening up of art to the masses. It is now generally accepted that everyone should have the ability to see and appreciate art works; this is one facet of the idea known as the 'democratisation of art'. An idea that was particularly pioneered by the Bauhaus.

Neither does art have to be work produced from valuable materials, such as bronze, which due to their intrinsic cost are inaccessible to many artists. This is the other half of the dualistic concept of 'the democratisation of art'. The idea that everybody should be able to access the tools and media to produce art.

1968 was the year the passions of the partners took hold of Troika. Benny too attempted to extend Troika's artistic breadth. Since Troika's inception he had harboured the idea of producing some hand thrown ware. This was soon abandoned due to the efficiencies of moulded production and the popularity of their new cast designs.

Benny saw an opportunity to use the name they had built to attract new buyers, to make new pots. Leslie was beginning to become the dominant influence at Troika and Benny naturally wanted to feel more involved in the creative side of things, as he had been at the beginning. He had worked so hard in expanding Troika though the marketing and business and now wanted more than just the day to day labour of packing the kiln and delivering to shops far and wide. After all, he was still a potter at heart and was itching to get his hands dirty again.

With this in mind Benny talent-spotted a young potter by the name of John Bedding. He had run away from a stifling home life in London for the freedom of St Ives and a job at the Arch Pottery run by Anthony Richards. John remembers,

"They were thinking of having a thrown line. They thought because I could throw I could help develop a thrown line. That was Benny's idea. It was Benny who asked me."

Unfortunately, like a seed cast upon rocky ground, the thrown side of Troika failed to emerge. Benny and John started working together but Benny's role in the day to day running of a now busy business took its toll. Lack of time meant the project lost impetus and was shelved. Most of the throwing John did went into moulded production,

"The throwing side of Troika never really developed. I used to throw for Leslie for making new moulds. You had to make the master mould first which was made of solid plaster. But in order to do that you had to model something in clay for the shape. So for the round ones, like the mugs, it was easier to throw."

As throwing was not a huge requirement, John began working in each department whenever a spare hand was required. He was unique in that respect, everyone else had their specific roles in the process. In the end John spent much more time with Leslie,

"I gravitated towards Leslie because Leslie was the creative one. When I first met Leslie he didn't like me much. It was in the Lion pub. He was sat at the bar with John Antrobus the playwright and they were pissed out of their heads. I was playing darts and at the time I had glasses, but tinted glasses, so it looked like I was playing darts with shades on. So they look up 'what the fuck, who are you?' They tore me to bits, even drunk they were pretty good at pulling people apart and I just felt that big. I was a little bit wary of him because of that. So when I went to Troika I kept my distance at first."

The Heal's exhibition and the attempt at a thrown range had raised issues about the future of Troika. John remembers how Benny and Leslie would often be in deep discussion,

"They did talk about the ethical value and the artistic value of things. I was a bit too young but Benny and Leslie had real conversations together so they would have said this sort of thing, they intellectualised a lot."

These conversations, which had been a key part of Troika's development, now began to take on a new tone and became arguments. Leslie wanted Troika to become sculptural, following the lead of the Heal's exhibition. Benny wanted more handmade objects with a sense of crafted individuality and utility. It was not only a clash of personal visions. Benny did not feel that the intensive production process, needed to produce pieces like "Sculptures for Living", could be economically viable. Roland saw it from the outside,

"I think that part of the fall out was because Leslie wanted to get really sculptural. He was fanatical over it. I remember the firings being critical. First time I had ever heard about soaking a kiln which is to reach temperature and keep it at that temperature for half an hour to an hour so the glaze really settled and those bubbles wouldn't be visible. Benny's argument was that they wouldn't become viable because they were too labour intensive."

In previous years Benny and Leslie had found common ground and agreements came easily. Decisions about what pieces to make and where to sell them were made and executed. Now, as the passions took hold, the two partners found it less simple to find a shared purpose, or perhaps were less willing to compromise. Judith remembers these disputes,

"Leslie didn't really discuss their relationship but I remember when I first knew Leslie, and you go to parties and things, Benny and Leslie were always arguing. This was in 1967/68. Leslie didn't want to discuss it. I don't know if it was the input of the designing or that Benny

"Leslie had a reputation; he took no prisoners really, especially when he'd had a drink."

John Bedding

wanted it to go more his way. I mean I think the reason it went the way it did was that the mould-made stuff was selling."

In the end it was to be Leslie's presence in the workshop and vociferous personality that prevailed. Leslie appeared to have made a decision and it was becoming impossible for Benny to get his ideas across. Troika never ventured into thrown ware again and distanced itself further from craft and utility by stopping production of most of the obviously domestic shapes, except for a few small exceptions like the 'mugs'.

John Bedding was one of the few career potters to ever work at Troika. He had wanted to be a potter since he saw a display of throwing clay on a school trip to the Isle of Wight. As there was no throwing to do he felt that he wasn't progressing towards this goal so after about a year he left to train at the Leach Pottery. John recalls that Leslie took this personally,

"They weren't very happy when I went to Leach, it was the enemy. It was the intellectual enemy. There was a lot of argument against that sort of brown pottery. I didn't massively respect the Leach Pottery I just saw it as a place I could train. I kept in touch with Benny; Leslie was the one who really didn't like me going to the Leach. Benny couldn't have cared less I don't think. Leslie really didn't speak to me after that. He would nod to me and maybe make a few snide remarks."

Troika did not continue with the "Sculptures for Living" pieces. Benny was right about the production costs and the market was not there. No matter how much of a creative salesman he was he found them difficult to sell. Heal's were only interested in a few small 'cubes' and 'bowls'. They were a home design shop after all, not a gallery. Things had to have some practical function. Benny didn't give up but decided to try Habitat, which was right next door to Heal's on Tottenham Court Road. Their taste seemed perfectly suited to the white ware but they refused it too. Their decision was not simply based upon whimsical taste but upon hard economics. Benny recalls,

"No one was buying the white stuff. I remember taking the big white 'ashtray' to Habitat and they discussed it. They said they'd let us know. I asked if they wanted to have a meeting about it but they said no. At that time suddenly there was an influx of Italian china, white and soft. If you look at Troika it has hard edges, we wanted it sharp. I didn't know anything about high fired biscuit and low fired glaze, which I do now. We should have done that in a way because that's the most economic. A lot of the Italian stuff came in very cheap, much cheaper than we could do it."

"Leslie was as soft as shit, but if he wanted his own way, he could make your life a bloody misery."
Judith Illsley

White glazed Apple

The only success of Troika's experiment with white glaze was the 'ashtray'. As it was very contemporary of the style and fashions of the late sixties, it began to be used as props in television shows. Benny remembers,

"The thing that really took off with the white stuff, apart for the little white ashtray, was the big one, the big white ashtray, and that took off because there was a firm somewhere near Baker Street, (London) and they gave us an order for thirty maybe forty of them and they were hiring them out. That's when they went on to the BBC as props."

Another success for that 'ashtray' came when Heal's were given the contract to refit Abbey Road Studios. As part of the refurbishment pieces of Troika were used to add a contemporary air. In 1969 the Beatles entered the studio for the last time. The album Let It Be was accompanied by a book called Get Back, featuring photographs of the recording sessions. The 'ashtrays' feature prominently in these pictures. Leslie was a huge fan of the Beatles and cast some apples, sending one white ceramic apple to each member of the Beatles. Apple of course being the Beatles' record label. It was never found out if they received them but at least here there was some evidence of just how close he had come to his heroes.

Chapter Eight

"I would say Leslie drew in clay. If you look at all the early Troika it will have no pattern on it, it will just be washed. Or with little bits picked out. Done for speed and quickness. Leslie was literally drawing in the clay at that time and then it started to develop itself."

– Roland Bence

Leslie continued to pursue the idea of sculpture through the textured pieces, where he could carve and model the clay to form abstract reliefs. These were imposed upon the sides of Troika's already interesting shapes; thus creating free-standing sculptures.

Although the argument between the partners seemed to have been won by Leslie, there was an element of compromise in the aftermath. Leslie could only justify making art if he could generate income from it. As he wasn't willing to go through the galleries it had to be through Troika. Thus he had to use Troika's already commercially viable shapes. Leslie was always seeking to distance himself from the idea of the utilitarian object because it apparently devalued the appreciation of the piece as art. This was an attitude he unconsciously shared with many artists who had experimented with ceramics, such as Picasso or Matisse. Sylvia noticed the swift change from glazed to textured,

"There was some textured around when I started but the most common things were the coffee sets and the mugs which were all glazed. There was a big crossover. 70% glazed and 30% textured at the start but the textured stuff came through very fast."

The new larger kiln meant that many of the early larger shapes could return to production. The 'double base vase' and the 'shoulder bottles' began to reappear. Where these pieces were once glazed or covered in dense, almost black oxides, now they were textured and decorated completely in the standard Troika palette of blue, green and fawn.

These new pieces were the culmination of every risk and experiment up to this point. There is a noticeable development in the complexity and composition of the textured shapes in 1968. They had become complete pieces of work, as if Leslie was conveying the same totality of idea as he would in one of his paintings. The sides now had intricate carving and moulding instead of lines almost randomly sliced into them. The decorators began to follow the forms in the clay rather than ignoring them.

This period was one of the most fruitful for Leslie. The 'shoulder bottles' no longer had the images of plaques pushed into them but had fresh designs held together with a genuine definite style. Their new sculptural features were now accentuated by the decoration rather than having almost random coloured shapes superimposed over the carved lines. This development can be best seen by comparing 'wheel vases' of this period to earlier examples.

At the same time these pieces showcase a new-found self-confidence from Leslie in his own natural abilities. Nothing was held back, his vision was uncorrupted by a need for acceptance. He had finally found his own form of freedom, perhaps inspired by new freedoms in his personal life.

When looking at Troika as an art form, it is easy to point to the white pieces and forget the textured. The 'Sculptures for Living' pieces fitted neatly into a paradigm, comparisons for which can be drawn from Ben Nicholson's work and contemporary sixties design, such direct comparisons being much harder to make with the textured pieces. With the Heal's pieces it is easy to see the conscious attempt to make art and the heady pleasures of objective achievement. Yet, by trying so hard these pieces did not have the same deftness as the textured-ware. Some of the individualism and the attractive rebellion was absent. Bryan thinks,

   "In this light it makes sense why the Heal's exhibition and the smooth ware was never as successful, it was not Leslie. It was Leslie trying to be something he professed to hate. Part of the establishment. The people who loved Troika loved the rebel."

The Heal's pieces are also considered as the most artistic representation of Troika's work as they remain as individual objects. This is only due to the fact that they sold poorly and so were never reproduced. If there was a market for them, Troika would have produced them in their thousands. However, if it is individuality and a unique style that makes 'good art', rather than an individual object, it is these new textured pieces which were the more successful.

With the benefit of hindsight the 'Sculptures for Living' pieces, although striking, seem the most dated of all of Troika's work. It was prescient of Troika to focus upon the textured ware, even if their hand was forced, rather than follow the Heal's pieces as Leslie so hoped to do. The textured pieces anticipated a new era and allowed Troika to further its growth.

The Heal's catalogues from this period demonstrate this change in taste. There is a distinct change in the décor and design of the rooms on display. The ethic is much more organic; natural rather than angular. The furniture became rounded and comfortable, rather than square and elegant. The objects placed amongst this furniture began to include historical artefacts, such as a Victorian globe or craftsman's tools, rather than solely cutting edge design. The textured Troika started to appear in the photos instead of the glazed ware.

The prevailing mood was that there was a sense of exploration, of trying to understand this new world that their generation had built; of integrating the old with the so very new. Textured Troika can be thought to embody both extremes, a feature which gives it a transcendental, timeless quality. It had the feel of the ancient with its rough stone-like façade. Yet this façade incorporated modern geometric patterns and unconscious archetypal sketches, abstract forms. It was easy for Heal's to take Troika's radical change of direction in their stride.

In the corner of the small studio at Wheal Dream, Leslie and Roland had been working closely together and had formed a bond. So in late 1968 Leslie invited Roland to try his hand at making moulds instead of just casting from them. Production was increasing and it was obvious that Roland found the whole process intriguing. It also seems that Leslie was excited to have an apprentice to show off to.

There was a collection of basic shapes made out of plaster, each one a master block. Now each one had a recess cut into it. When a new mould was made this recess would be filled with a mixture of sand and slip. When this had begun to dry, a pattern would then be carved into it or modelled up out of it. This allowed a repetitive process to have some flexibility for change and development and is another factor which explains the breadth of Troika's designs.

Casting is a corrosive process and so the plaster moulds were only capable of about twenty castings before they needed to be replaced. Roland's new job was to take Leslie's master block, cast a copy of it, called the 'master double'. He would then use this to make replica moulds. This process eventually wore out the master too, so new masters were also constantly needed. With each new master came a new design. Roland said,

"I learnt how to make moulds, but only the repeats. Leslie would make a master then I would cast them and make them from there, I would make three from his masters. About twenty casts and they were pretty knackered. Some of the pots were adapted so that we could paint texture on them so they would last longer."

The deterioration of the moulds had initiated the idea of texturing and provided opportunity for continual development. Perhaps if the moulds were made of a more substantial material Troika would not have produced such a large range of work.

It wasn't only Roland that Leslie taught. He was invited to run a course at Redruth Art School in the summer term of 1969. He taught a class for one day a week. He showed them how to make moulds and how to set up a business. Leslie was popular with the students because he would take them to the pub at lunch time.

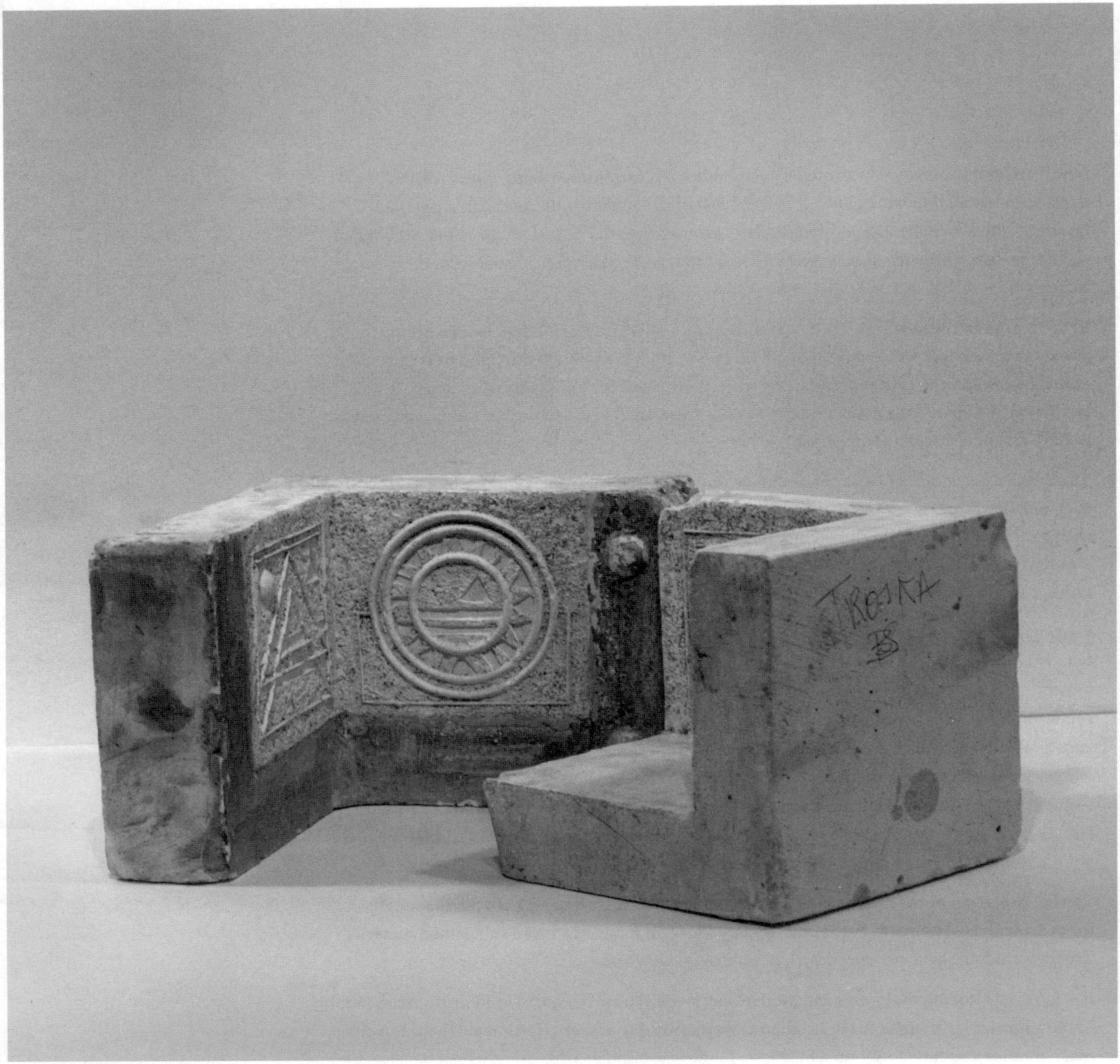

Small 'cube' mould

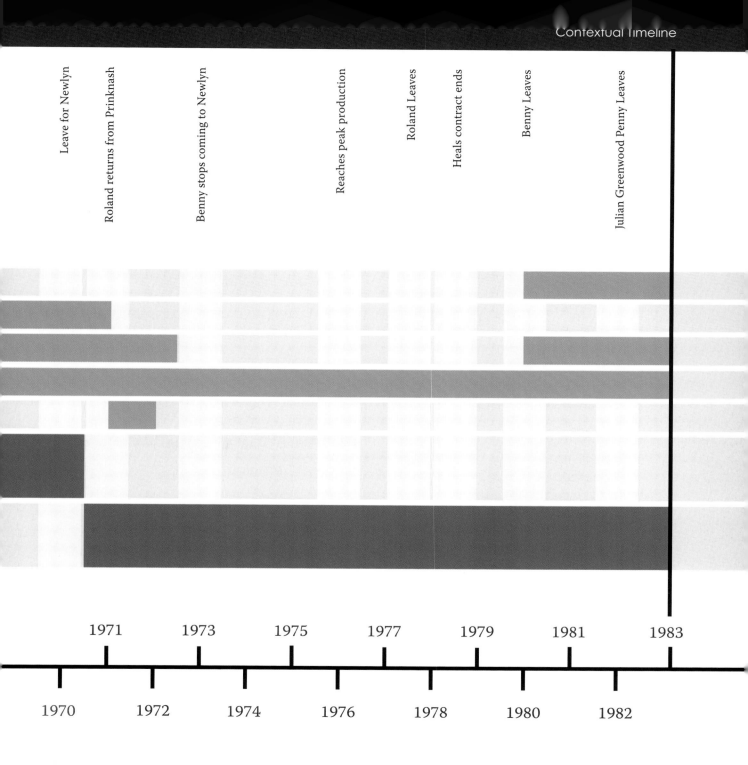

Leave for Newlyn

Roland returns from Prinknash

Benny stops coming to Newlyn

Reaches peak production

Roland Leaves

Heals contract ends

Benny Leaves

Julian Greenwood Penny Leaves

1971   1973   1975   1977   1979   1981   1983

1970   1972   1974   1976   1978   1980   1982

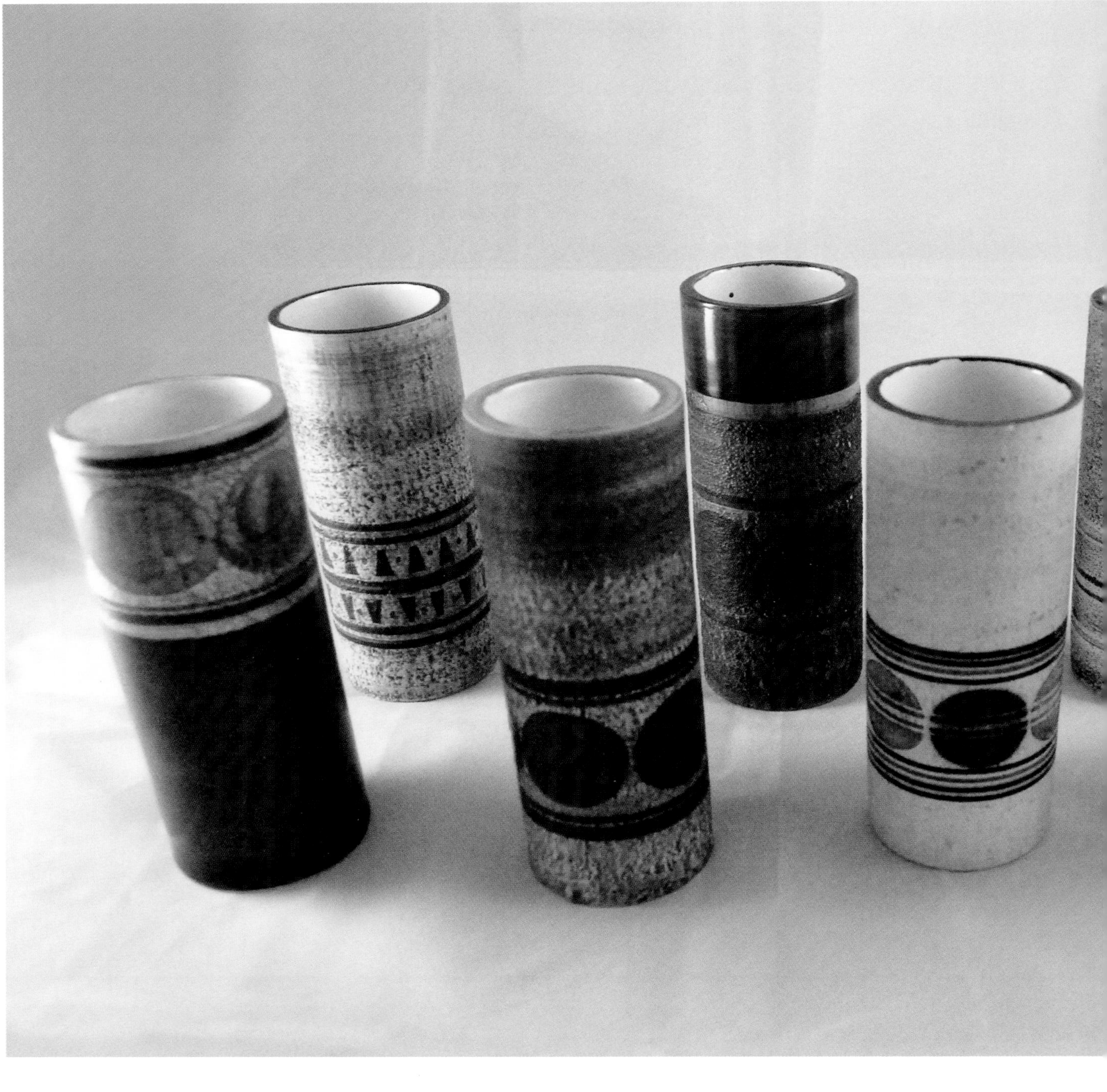

17. Selection of small cylinder vases –

Left to right: *Sylvia Valance c. 1967, Leslie King c. 1973, Honor Perkins c. 1968, Early St Ives Stamp, Leslie King c. 1973, Jane Fitzgerald c. 1981, Ruth Larratt c. 1973, Anne Lewis c. 1972.*

18. 'Pillar' – Designed by Leslie Illsley, decorated by Anne Lewis, c. 1972

19. 'Anvil' – Original shape by Leslie Illsley, featured pieces designed by Roland Bence.
Decorated by Annette Waters (left) and Alison Brigden (right), c. 1977

20. 'Spice jar' – Designed by Leslie Illsley, decorated by Annette Waters, c. 1981

21. Troika range, 1973

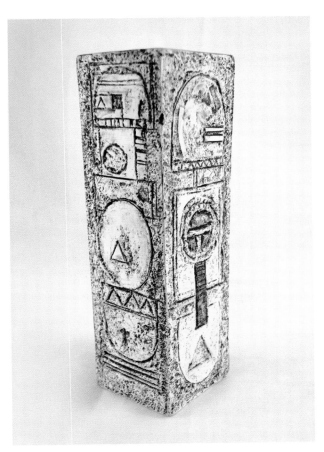

22. Large 'cuboid' vase –
Designed by Leslie Illsley, decorated by Anne Lewis, c. 1972

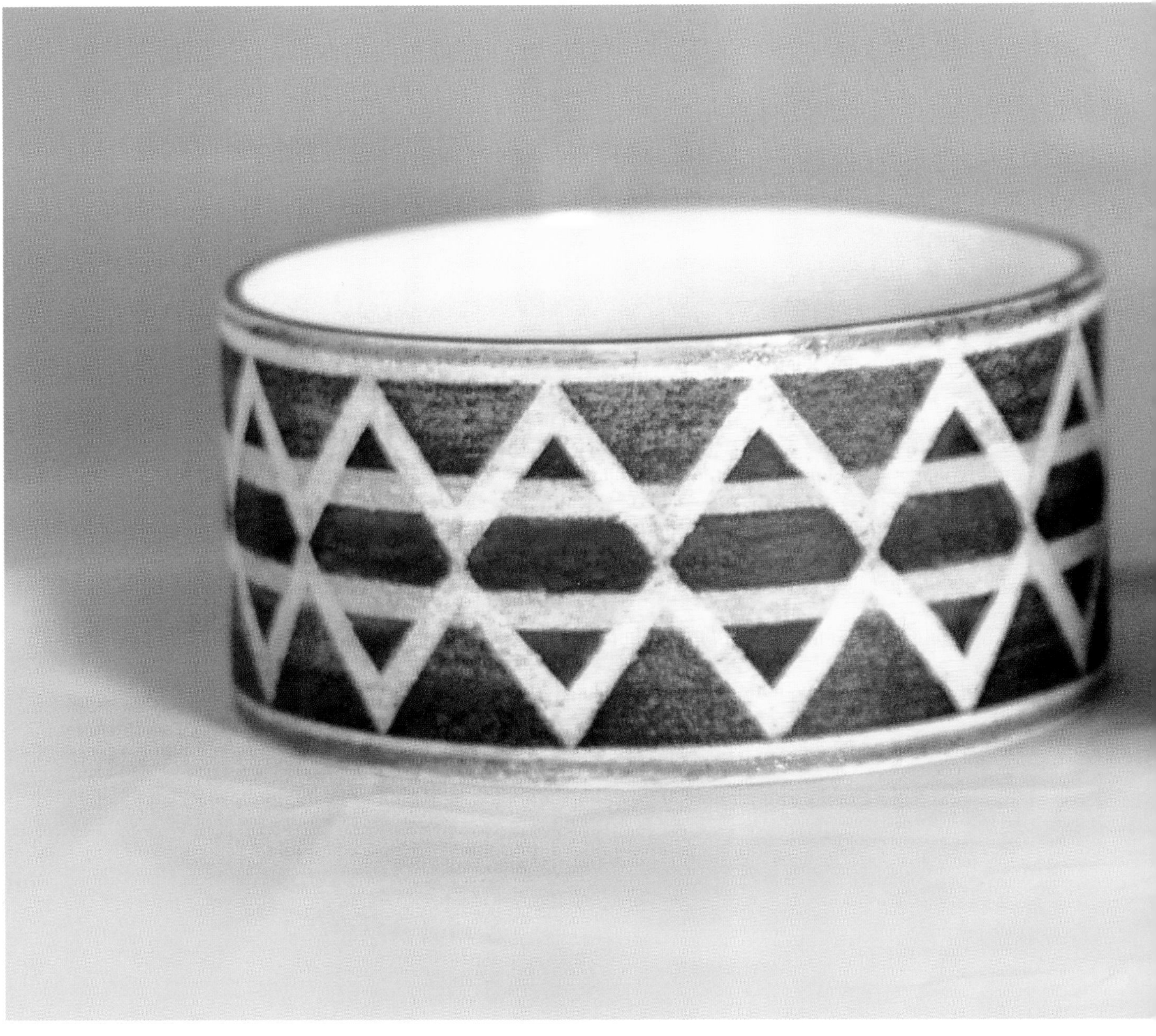

23. Drum bowls – Designed by Benny Sirota, decorated by Jane Fitzgerald (left), Louise Jinks (right) late 70's

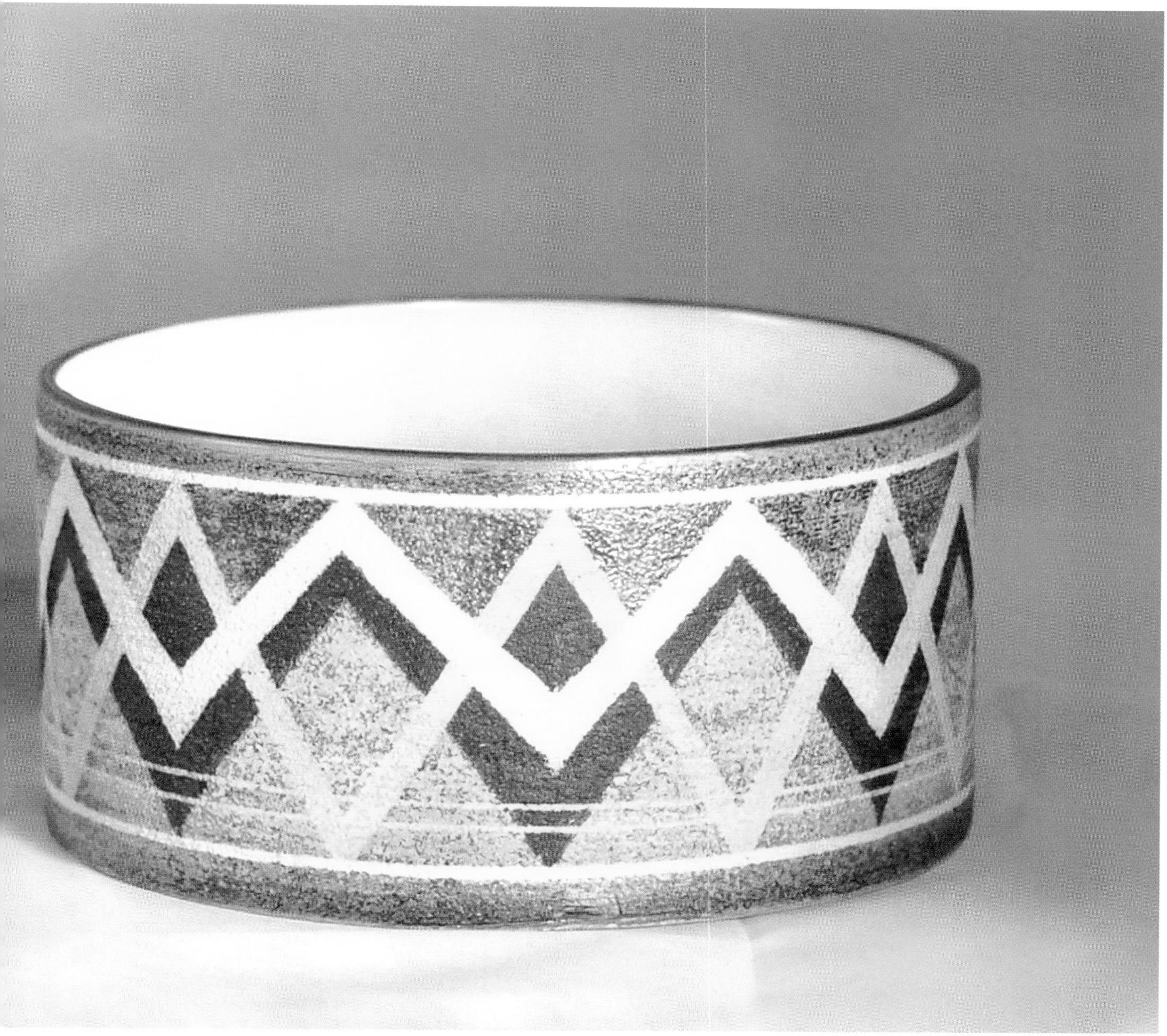

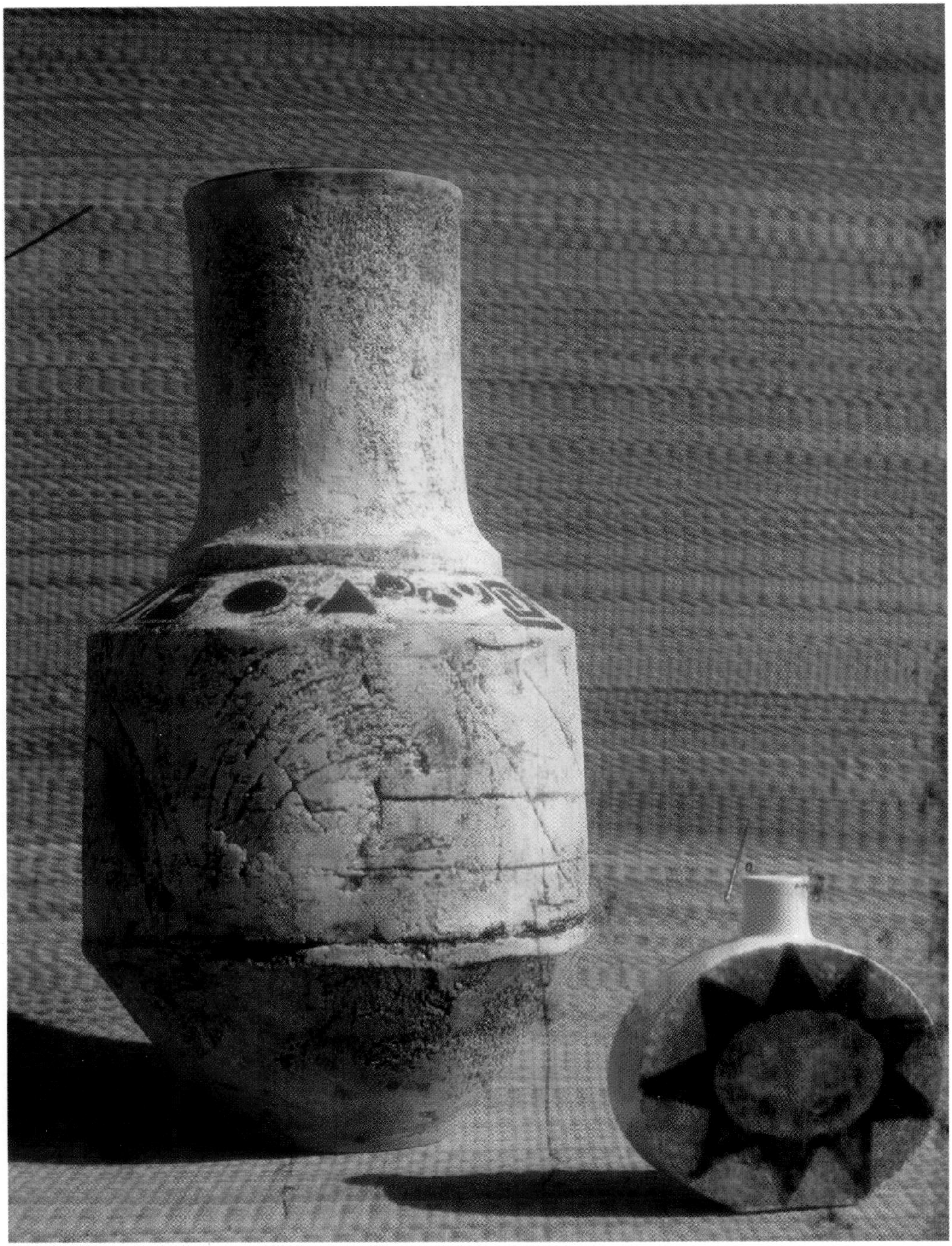

24. Far left:
Urn and Perfume
bottle, c. 1963

25. Urn Decorated by
Jane Fitzgerald, c. 1981

Artist Monograms

B

.... Mary Baker

September 1976 – November 1976

.... Avril Bennett

May 1976 – August 1979 (See Avril Pellow)

.... John Bedding

1967 – 1968

.... Teo Bernatowicz

March 1973 – April 1975

.... Roland Bence

1966 – c. 1969 & November 1971 – c. 1978

.... David Bridge

c. 1969

.... Sally Bench

February 1975 – December 1975

.... Alison Brigden

April 1977 – June 1983

No monogram .... Stella Benjamin

March 1963 – October 1967
(Stella worked at Troika before they used monograms. It is likely
Stella used 'Troika St Ives' on the bottom of her pieces.)

.... Penny Broadribb

October 1973 – August 1976

C

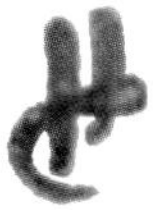

Honor Curtis

c. 1969 – April 1974 (See Honor Perkins)

D

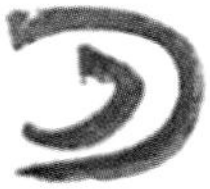

Tina Doubleday

February 1977 – November 1978

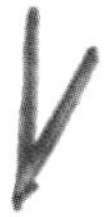

Vicky Drew

April 1981 – October 1981

E

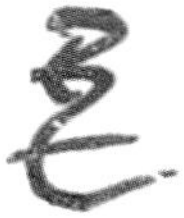

Beverly Elwood

October 1973 – May 1974

F

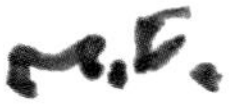

Maureen Fyffe

June 1975 – August 1975

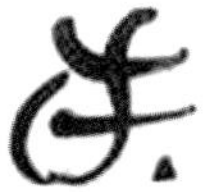

Jane Fitzgerald

May 1978 – June 1983

G

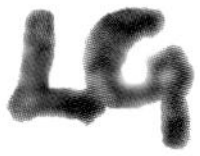

Louise Graham

December 1976 – January 1977

H

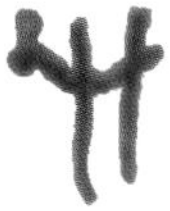

Linda Hazel

September 1971 – April 1973

I

.... Judith Illsley (nee Howard)
August 1979 – June 1983

.... Leslie Illsley
March 1963 – November 1983

J

.... Holly Jackson
July 1977 – January 1978

.... Louise Jinks
September 1976 – May 1981

.... Anne Jones
October 1975 – August 1979

.... Penny Ellis Jones
c. 1971 – November 1971

K

.... Sue Kewell
June 1974 – January 1975

.... Simone Kilburn
July 1975 – April 1977

.... Leslie King

November 1971 – June 1972

L

.... Ruth Larratt

November 1971 – May 1972

.... Anne Lewis

c. 1969 – June 1974

.... Sue Lowe

January 1976 – July 1976

M

.... M Murrell

July 1974 – June 1975

P

.... CP

July 1973 – August 1973

.... Marilyn 'Murphy' Pascoe

c. 1968 – September 1973

.... Avril Pellow

August 1973 – May 1976 (See Avril Bennett)

P

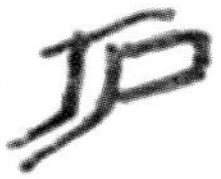

Julian Penny
June 1977 – October 1982

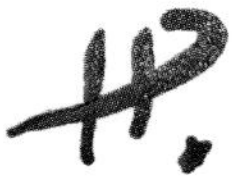

Honor Perkins
October 1967 – c. 1969 (See Honor Curtis)

R

No monogram .... Kristen Roth
March 1963 – 1965
(Kristen worked at Troika before they used monograms. It is likely Kristen used 'Troika St Ives' on the bottom of her pieces.)

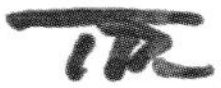

Tamsin Ruhrmund
September 1979 – February 1980

S

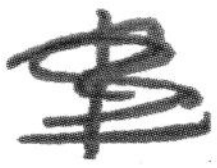

Benny Sirota
March 1963 – c. 1980

T

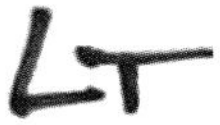

Linda Taylor
July 1971 – April 1973

V

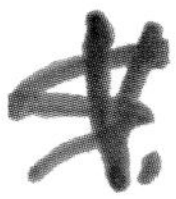

Sylvia Valance
October 1966 – December 1970

28. Giant 'wheel vase', designed by Leslie Illsley decorated by Alison Brigden, c. 1981

29. 'Column,' lamp base –
Designed by Leslie Illsley,
decorated by Eleanor Winning
c. 1974

Don Fowler was employed at Troika to help with the casting and fettling now that Roland was making moulds. Don was an instant hit with his fellow workers. According to Honor, Don was "a brilliant guitarist, he used to bring his guitar in and jam at lunch times. It was fantastic."

As the business continued to expand two new decorators, Anne Lewis and Marilyn 'Murphy' Pascoe, were also employed, taking the number of decorators up to four.

During breaks in work or in the evenings, Leslie would always actively encourage his staff to experiment and show off their own artistic side. There were kilns, glazes, clay and oxides available and they were free to use them. He was always equally keen to make the point that whatever work was made in the staff's own time was theirs and not 'Troika'. Judith explains that Leslie didn't want the workers to take advantage of using the established Troika name,

"He said that people could do things but they couldn't call it 'Troika'. The facilities are there, the kilns are there, the clay is there, the decorating materials are there. If you want to make your own stuff, do it, I'm not going to charge you. But it's not 'Troika', it comes under your own name. Yet lots of things have been sold as 'Troika', because they had been made in the factory but they are not 'Troika'."

This was a generous opportunity but one that few actively pursued. John recalls,

"Your own artistic ideas were encouraged a little bit at Troika. I had a wheel there I could go and work on at night. Benny would put them in the kiln, but I didn't really have the ethic to do that. It was St Ives, it was the sixties. I was out at night!"

Roland made the most of this chance to utilise the space and the equipment,

"Leslie was really good to me at the beginning he said 'if there are gaps in the kiln you can use them'. So I used to make bits and pieces to sell in the shop. In the early days I attempted stuff on the wheel, then I decorated them. They were really rough, I never threw much. Maybe when John Bedding was there I got influenced. It was a crap wheel, you could never throw anything properly unless you got used to it. I kept asking Leslie to change it but he refused to have anything to do with it. Leslie told me off for putting 'Troika' on the bottom of my stuff. He said you can make pieces, but don't put 'Troika' on it."

Roland and Don went on to develop a larger range of goods that used more familiar Troika production techniques to supplement their wages. Roland remembers,

"In St Ives I also made a lot of chess sets, I made hundreds of them. I sold them to friends and through the showroom in St Ives. They didn't pay me much so that's how they kind of justified it. I doubled my wages when I was making those. It was never seen as detracting

"I learnt how to make moulds, but only the repeats. Leslie would make a master then I would cast them and make them from there, I would make three from his masters..."
Roland Bence

from what Troika was doing. There was a certain amount of independence. Don and I were making these rings. We were selling thousands, we were down there late and we had so many orders we could have filled a whole kiln but Leslie wouldn't let us. He'd say you're only allowed to fill the little spaces in between the pots. These were definitely not sold as 'Troika', he said you keep that separate from 'Troika'."

In 1969 an interesting potential opportunity for major international expansion literally walked into the showroom. Benny recalled,

"We had some guys come over, Americans, and they bought some pots, quite a lot, and they left us this card. They were called the Virginia Glass Company. Then they wrote us a letter to ask if we would consider moving over to the States and making Troika at their factory in Virginia. I don't think either Leslie or I were very keen on the idea. I said, and I'm so glad I did, 'look, before you decide on that, give us an order, we'll send it over and see how it goes.' They never sold a thing. Leslie said 'you were right, not the American scene'. So we didn't go to Virginia."

Roland would have been the one to go to America and set it all up, "I was off to America, Leslie was arranging for me to go over there to show them how to make the shapes but it never materialised."

Since he had begun to make moulds, Roland had been slowly raising his profile within the company. Conversations were being had about the potential of him becoming a partner. But he was beginning to get frustrated as these conversations were never actualised. This all came to a head when the American opportunity fell through.

A pattern was emerging. Roland was constantly being asked to take on more and more responsibility but the opportunity to become a partner never manifested. He felt under-appreciated and fed up. He had his own future to consider. It all ended in the autumn of 1969 when Roland had a huge row with Leslie and stormed out,

"Right at the beginning he would say, 'Keep at it and you'll be a partner', Benny even said it once. When I started making moulds he promised me a partnership. But then said he couldn't do it. I had a steaming row with Leslie about partnerships.

That's what it was like for me. They would go, 'you're gonna do this, you're gonna do that…' and I had this row with Leslie and so did the same with him as I did with my first job, I said I'm off.

"I had this row with Leslie and so did the same with him as I did with my first job, I said I'm off."

Roland Bence

He called me every name under the sun and said I was abandoning him. He could be quite manipulative. We'd had a good crack, it was a laugh. We had rows but that is all part of the fair but I wanted to expand."

Troika employed Ian Draper, a former hairdresser, to replace Roland. There was no time to think about what might have been, bigger issues were knocking at the door of the studio at Wheal Dream. Pop Short had sold the building to St Ives Town Council. A letter arrived from them saying that they would not be extending the lease, which had expired. It had already been over five years since Troika took over from Powell and Wells.

The council, having already taken over the Seaman's Mission upstairs to build a museum, planned to extend this to the downstairs part of the building. Suddenly there was a real sense that their time in Wheal Dream was up. Benny was not very happy with the decision,
   "We never wanted to leave, we were kicked out by the council, I was furious I went and 'bollocked' this bloke from the council, really lost my temper."

Although they were forced out, the time was right to leave. Troika was a growing enterprise and it needed bigger premises to continue the expansion. In fairness the council had not completely abandoned them, they were offered a place on Penbeagle Industrial Estate, located just off Higher Stennack, where the town gives way to the cold moor and the coast road begins its roller-coaster journey to Lands End. St Ives is a small town, but the estate felt like a million miles away from the central hub-bub of the harbour and the pubs. They may have still been in St Ives but they would be consigned to the edge, far away from the scene, from life and action. Not only that but it would have been prominent in their minds that Penbeagle was right next door to Bernard Leach's pottery. Judith comments,
   "Leslie wanted to be in St Ives, where he could just walk along the road to the pub, where you could meet people. He was very social, a very social animal, he didn't want to be stuck up some industrial estate somewhere. I mean he was a free spirit, he wanted to feel free."

If Penbeagle was unacceptable there were no other suitable locations in St Ives. Buildings in St Ives were expensive and large buildings rare. Every spare square foot had been turned into a bed and breakfast or a summer let. So they were forced to look for premises further afield, all over Penwith. They soon found a large run-down warehouse in Newlyn, an industrial fishing port on the other side of the Cornish peninsula, just beside Penzance.

Properties were much cheaper in Newlyn as it wasn't a tourist destination. Benny discovered an added financial bonus in moving there, an area where regeneration was being encouraged. He contacted COSIIRA, a rural development scheme and was able to secure a development loan for the purchase of premises in Newlyn. This was much cheaper than getting a loan from the bank. Funnily enough COSIIRA were part of Rural Industries and so were exactly the same people who had given him his pottery prize all those years ago.

Although a move out of St Ives was now confirmed, Troika was able to maintain a base there. Since 1968, Troika had been selling to a shop on Fore Street run by Peter Rowe. Judith worked there for a season in 1968. In 1969 Peter wanted to move on so Troika took over the lease. This fitted in with Benny's sales plan where they wouldn't sell to more than one shop in a town; a plan that maintained exclusivity. It made sense that the one shop in St Ives should be run by Troika, especially now that the business was expanding.

The disagreements of the last year were still in the air so the shop provided a way for each partner to have a base from which to run their side of the expanding operation. Leslie was running the studio and now Benny had the shop. It gave the partners some much needed respite from each other and allowed them to relax and appreciate what they had already achieved together and what they still hoped to accomplish.

Opposite page: Small 'cube' mould

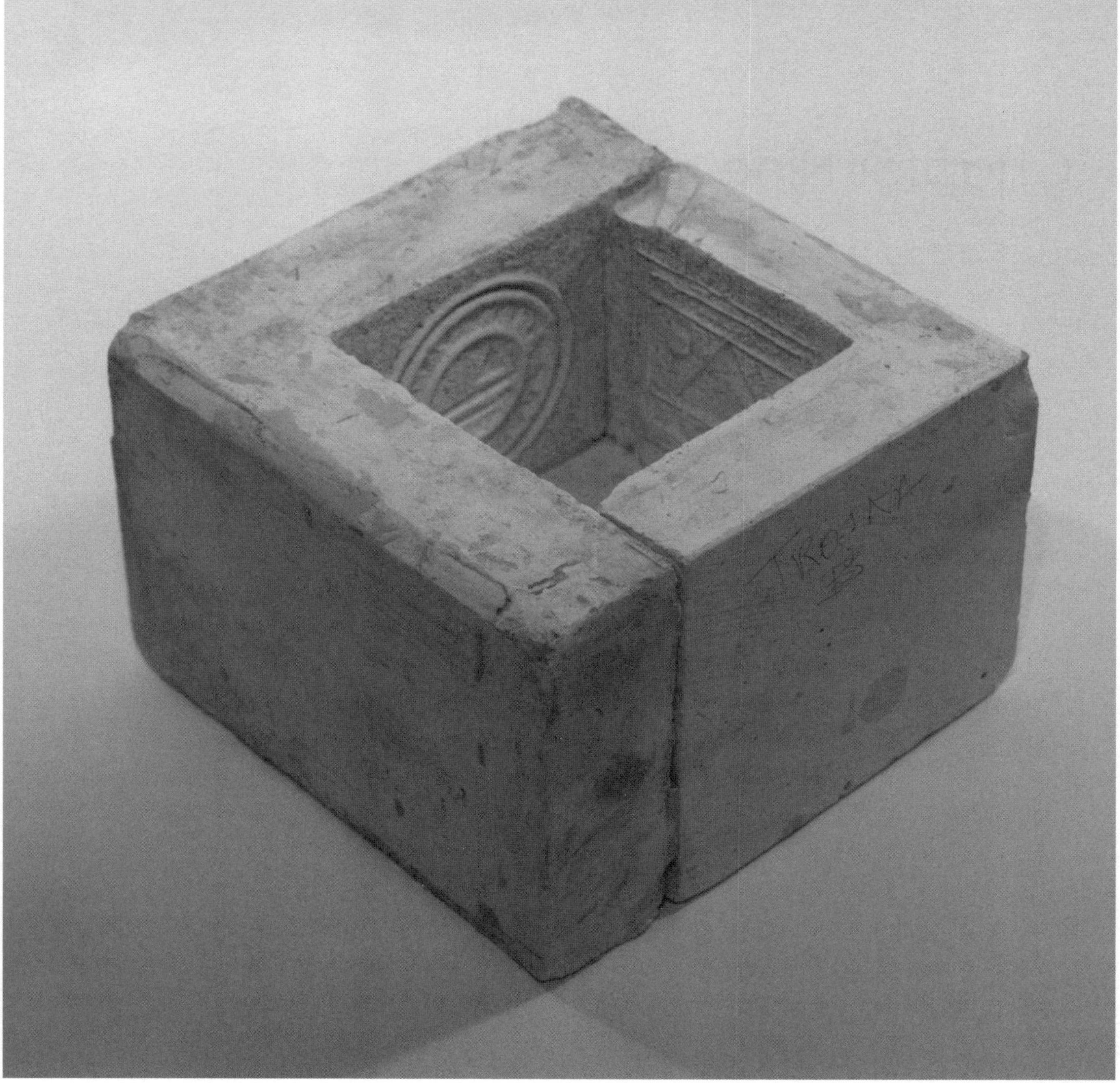

Chapter Nine

"...It was in Newlyn that we really got busy."

- Benny Sirota

In 1970, Newlyn was a thriving fishing port. Although only ten miles from St Ives as the crow flies, the two places had little in common. Newlyn still retained its relatively close-knit, mainly Methodist, community at that time. The sea was hidden behind the fish market and the harbour walls, in St Ives the blue water trailed off into the distance. In Newlyn huge trawlers lined up side by side to offload their catches, in St Ives little skiffs rocked calmly in the bay.

Newlyn's harbour was not only a base for its thriving fishing fleet but also serviced the nearby Penlee Quarry. Its shops were functional and few, unlike the variety of gift shops in St Ives that catered for the tourists. Shadowed by its neighbour, Penzance, it struggled to keep its own identity. There were few jobs available to the locals, other than in the fishing or quarry industries, as tourism had not arrived there.

The fishermen were of a different breed to St Ives. They were the hard men of the sea, who not only had to fight the elements but the complexities of commercial fishing. The fishing industry in St Ives was, by now, mainly confined to tourists hiring boats. In Newlyn it was day to day life.

The dreams in Newlyn were more realistic and down to earth, not like the ethereal dreams that washed over St Ives and gave it such a serene quality. Where St Ives was washed clean in winter, Newlyn hunched up and confronted the storms with stoic intensity, unmoved by nature, respectful of its dominance. Benny put it neatly, "Newlyn was a working place."

New investment was needed in Newlyn. A lot of empty buildings were left as the fishing industry had decreased. The new premises that Benny and Leslie had bought for £2600 was one of those empty buildings. It was once a salting house where pilchards were salted until the devastating decline in pilchard shoals around the beginning of the twentieth century meant this industry declined with it and eventually ceased to exist. The building was hidden up a tiny side street called Fradgan Place.

The access wasn't ideal as the buildings and roads were built long before motorised transport, the Troika van just about squeezed through. The streets are still cobbled in the area of the Fradgan even today. The small, quaint cottages in the Fradgan were built specifically to service the fishermen and their families. It was peaceful, only a minute away from the bustling harbour; and apart from the constant smell it was easy to forget it was next door to a large fishing port.

The street may have been small but the building was huge. More than four times the size of the space they had occupied at Wheal Dream, which made it ideal for expansion. This time the building was owned by the company so the future was more assured.

It didn't take Leslie and Benny long to find a local. Just two minutes walk from Fradgan Place was a pub called the Swordfish. But, like everything else in Newlyn, the pubs were different to St Ives. The Swordfish was a fisherman's pub mainly frequented by the locals. It was somewhere where their ancestors had relaxed for many generations before them. Leslie felt at home here. He felt an affinity for it. He had fallen out with the pretence of the art scene and there was little pretence in Newlyn. Work and the sea dominated life leaving little room for whimsy. Benny could see the business potential but did not feel so fond of their new home; he identified more with the craft and banter of St Ives, he recalls,

"Leslie never went back to St Ives, he drank in Newlyn. I think he liked Newlyn because Newlyn had fishermen there, which in St Ives was on the way out. You know Leslie, he was an argumentative bastard, especially when he had one too many. I don't know why, he just was. The fishermen sort of tolerated it, they liked him, he was a bright lad. I say lad, man."

Although Newlyn was predominantly a working place it had an art heritage of its own. The Newlyn School had been a major contributor to Victorian painting and the Newlyn Art Gallery stands in testament to that. The turn of the twentieth century heralded the emergence of Newlyn copper and jewellery-making as an alternative income to fishing. More recently, Newlyn had continued to attract industrial types of creative businesses. There were two large potteries, Celtic Pottery, run by Maggie Fisher, and Tremaen, run by Angus Ellery, his son Peter and his daughter Brenda. There was also studio potter Eric Leaper who ran the Leaper Pottery. Where St Ives was dominated by the individual, Newlyn was all about the group.

Troika had always been a group endeavour and appreciated the acceptance they found in Newlyn. They are often talked about in the same terms as their counterparts here and perhaps their work is misunderstood because of this. Troika were different from these other enterprises in their attitude and outlook. Each Troika piece was produced as a limited run for the life of the mould and then independently decorated, making it rare for two pieces to be the same. The other manufacturers were potteries in the traditional sense and were concerned with producing ranges defined by a common theme.

However, all of these manufacturers shared a desire to make money. Money, or the acquisition of it through endeavour, is often a dirty concept in conversations about art. Troika was never scared of making money and this objective competition, won by results, suited them much more than the rivalries of taste and jealousy which an artistic community can cultivate. A community like St Ives, which in the sixties shunned the collective in favour of promoting the mythical personality of various lone figures.

It has been told that Leslie always wanted to ride through St Ives in a Rolls-Royce. This dream was not about wanting to be rich but just to prove to them all he was successful. Even if he had, it is unlikely this extravagant display would have had the impact he desired.

Fradgan Place had potential but it still had lugworms in the basement and salt in the walls. A local architect was brought in to draw up new plans for the building. It was to be completely overhauled. The middle of the three floors, which had been used to press the pilchards, was completely removed. Its ceiling was too low to be practical. As had been done at Wheal Dream, the front of the building was redesigned to provide a small showroom. The old metal hook that hung outside the upstairs loading bay was kept. Judith reminisced, "Leslie liked it, he thought it was industrial."

The medium sized biscuit kiln and the big kiln were brought from St Ives. A second big kiln was also then purchased. Sylvia remembers how before they moved in they helped to give it a final lick of paint,

"It wasn't too bad the transition, we all went over and painted and decorated the walls. Well we were painting anyway. It was basically tidying up. Benny used to pick us up at the Royal Cinema and drive us over in the little green Mini van."

With all these changes the building work took quite a long time. Troika finally moved in during September 1970. All of the staff went with them to Fradgan Place, Honor, Sylvia, Don, Anne, Murphy and Ian Draper. Don soon took over the responsibility of driving as he lived on the top of the hill on the way out of St Ives, towards Carbis Bay.

After Troika moved to Newlyn it became much more business like. There was more space in the kilns and more orders to be filled. Sylvia noticed a difference in atmosphere,

"The atmosphere did change when we moved to Newlyn... In a business sense, they seemed to be under much more pressure to get orders and to get things done."

Sylvia Valance

"The atmosphere did change when we moved to Newlyn, they seemed to be under much more pressure in Newlyn. In a business sense, they seemed to be under much more pressure to get orders and to get things done. I mean it was still really great to work there. That relaxed atmosphere you had in St Ives it didn't follow over to Newlyn."

The change in environment coupled with the commute ushered in other changes. Life was beckoning for some of these young decorators and Sylvia left for Australia in December 1970. She was replaced by Linda Taylor. Honor taught Linda but, as she was recently married, soon left to have a baby. Penelope Ellis-Jones was brought in to replace Honor.

When Troika moved, Leslie and Judith followed the business by moving to Mousehole, a tiny, former fishing village with a walled harbour, a short bus ride from Newlyn. This was never to be permanent. They lived there for six months in a cheap winter let whilst they looked for a house. As neither of them drove Leslie took the bus to work. Judith soon passed her test and they bought a small car which she then used to drive Leslie in to work, which she describes, "It was a Fiat and it was rubbish, it kept breaking down."

Leslie wanted to move to Penzance but Judith had other ideas. There were too many pubs in too small an area in Penzance. She was subtly directing a move to a more settled way of life, away from the chaos that followed Leslie through his twenties in St Ives. They eventually bought a large rambling house next to a farm, in Trewellard, a tiny hamlet on the coast road to St Ives. Wild parties changed to dinner parties. There were no distractions out at Trewellard and Judith drove Leslie to work every morning through the peaceful, often misty, moorland. The house was put into Judith's name as Leslie didn't want to feel tied down. He claimed to hate possessions and wanted "to be free of earthly goods". The only thing he ever really owned was his share in Troika, his life's work.

For Benny, things were different; he had been calling St Ives his home for longer than Leslie. He was older and had become part of the community. It was too much to just leave. Benny had his own friends and enjoyed the gentle harmony of the arts in St Ives, he didn't have any interest in, or perverse calling to, the harsh realities of Newlyn. He kept his house out at Cripplesease, perfectly situated between Newlyn and St Ives. To work there would be one thing but to live there completely another as he explains,

"We did have a lifestyle. It was really nice, there was the sea, it was great. Even though we were much busier and very successful, Newlyn was definitely not St Ives. I missed St Ives."

"We did have a lifestyle. It was really nice, there was the sea, it was great. Even though we were much busier and very successful, Newlyn was definitely not St Ives. I missed St Ives."
Benny Sirota

Troika was starting to make a serious amount of money. It had come a long way from the mid sixties when Leslie and Benny had celebrated long into the night upon deciding to pay themselves £20 a week in wages. Benny remembers it well,

"Leslie and I went out and got pissed one night, absolutely paralytic, which I don't usually do. We had decided we were going to draw £20 a week wages each. Big moment. A thousand pounds a year, which was a lot of money in those days. You could go out and have a night out for 2 and 6. You don't know what that is do you?"

Now they were able to do much more. Troika had provided enough financial security to allow Benny to get a mortgage to buy Giew House in 1966 and now had done the same for Leslie. Money seemed plentiful; the business owned two cars and the new factory at Newlyn. There was even some surplus money in the bank. Their accountant suggested that instead of having it sat in an account making the bank money they should invest it. The advice was taken and the company invested in a house on Penrose Terrace in Penzance. Judith remembers,

"They were lovely houses, just by the railway station, we left it empty for a few years, we were supposed to do it up or rent it out."

Troika was paving the way for a stable life for its partners, with all the trimmings. Leslie and Judith even had enough income to take a holiday. They didn't know where to go so Benny suggested Spain. So they took off for a month-long road trip in October of 1971. It was the first holiday Leslie had had since starting the business and he thoroughly appreciated the break.

Troika's expansion was part of Penwith's artistic growth during the early seventies. The whole peninsula now maintained a large arts industry that went far beyond St Ives. Many artists including Breon O'Casey, Dennis Mitchell and Bryan Wynter were to move out of St Ives during this period. St Ives was changing and they could now only find the same solitude and beauty they had fallen in love with in places like Paul or Botallack.

Chapter Ten

"People would say 'well they don't make cups and saucers! Don't make tea-sets!' I always think apart from the mugs and a few things that were usable, they are sculptures, little sculptures. I would never think to put flowers in them."

– Avril Bennett

The new workshop in Fradgan Place was much bigger; there was space to have specific areas for casting, fettling, packing and decorating. These areas were spread across two floors. On the ground floor there was a small office and a small showroom. In the back were the kilns and the storage shelves. Here the men, Benny, Leslie, Don and Ian worked.

In-between the bisque and second firing, trays of Troika would be placed on a rickety conveyor belt which took them upstairs to be decorated. There was now a whole floor available for the decorators to use rather than the single cramped table in St Ives, surrounded by dust and bags of clay. Large desks were pushed together, around which the decorators would sit and chat, listening to Radio One or various interesting records Leslie would bring in.

For the first year in Newlyn, Leslie was the only person at Troika making moulds. In order to keep up with the intensified production, some of the work was outsourced to a local mould-maker so Leslie only had to produce the masters. He also had other jobs to do, apart from mould-making. As manager of the workshop he had always looked after the staff and their wages. On 9th of July 1971 Leslie began a wage book. This fantastic piece of primary evidence was salvaged by Judith. Until recently, no-one else has seen it. It is a treasure trove of information and lists everyone who worked at Troika from 1971 until it closed. Including their start and finish dates and weekly wages. From it, the monograms of Troika's staff can be accurately assigned to each name and subsequently the pieces of Troika can be accurately dated. Other information can also be gleaned from this wage book, such as a picture of the overall health of the company, if it is assumed the total cost of weekly wages is proportional to weekly sales, for example.

It is observable from the wages book that staff members finishing their three-month probationary period were given a pay rise. This helped to retain staff in what was a highly skilled process, where time and money had been invested by the company. Other noticeable trends were that wage increases occurred almost every three months.

The wage book itself is neat and accurate. It was in continuous use for 13 years which gives us an insight into a different side of Leslie's character. His bookkeeping skills might be seen as somewhat at odds with his wild man artist image. But underneath all the bluster Leslie was a very conscientious practical man. Troika would not have existed for so long without the practical abilities of the partners.

The production of Troika's artistic work required Leslie to be multi-skilled, he had to make moulds and sculpt. But it didn't stop there, in order for Leslie to make money he had to divide time between creative and administrative roles. He had to respond to intuitive, unconscious drives but also to halt these occasionally to fill out a wage book or tax return.

John Bedding, former employee at Troika and now a self-employed potter, offers an insight,

"Being creative isn't the be all and end all. Being good at business is a pretty important thing. It depends how big an operation you want, the best way is to build a team but if you're a loner like me you have to do the whole lot. I mean every year I have to do my accounts. It's just torturous, I see these figures and they're just meaningless but it's too expensive to employ someone so I have to do it."

Leslie dealt with this conflicting existence admirably as is wonderfully illustrated by the fact that most of the receipts, bills and catalogues that remain today are covered in sketches and doodles, many representing finished pieces of Troika. However, the wage book is void of all additional art; there is only column after column of numbers. He took staff relations and wages very seriously and Benny was happy to leave him to it,

"Leslie was very, very good with them, the running of the pottery was his. He got on well with the staff; he got on well with everybody... Leslie handled everybody much better than I did. He was much more laid back about it. I could get up tight about it. You know, 'why haven't we got all those pots out because I've got to go and deliver them', I just left it all to Leslie and he was fine with them. Never pushed them. I would just say 'we need...' and he would say 'we'll get them done' or something and they just got done."

The working hours were steady but relaxed. The men would be in at about eight in the morning, the decorators at around nine. They all worked until five, Monday to Friday and had the weekends off. Leslie would often be in on Saturdays as well. He loved being in the place.

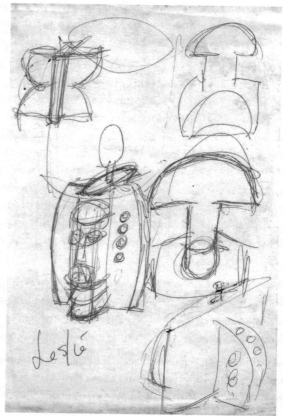

Sketch by Leslie of the 'mask' and 'anvil', in biro on the back of a catalogue

The autumn of 1971 marked Troika's first wave of employment in Newlyn. Leslie King, Ruth Larratt and Linda Hazel were all local to Newlyn. As things got busier Honor, always revered for her skill, was also asked back after her pregnancy. She worked for Troika from home, part-time but sometimes came into the workshop to train the new starters. Troika had left St Ives with four decorators, in July 1971 there were five and by September there were six. There were always two male members of staff who handled the casting and fettling, this number had remained constant since 1968.

Ruth Larratt was one of the first people employed in Newlyn. She had met Benny at a party and wanted a winter job; Troika was one of the few places open.

Although the atmosphere may have been more business-like in Newlyn, the same sense of belonging was still cultivated and the same freedoms were encouraged in the decoration. The atmosphere was what kept people at Troika, not the wages. Small gestures often went a long way, beyond what money could achieve. Ruth remembers that she got to keep the first piece she decorated,

"I did feel part of something there. I started deviating from the circles, got bored. Making up all my own patterns. All these lines and circles what else can we do. I never recall measuring anything. As long as it was in that format you were allowed to experiment. As long as it wasn't flowers! I never asked if I could do something different, I just did it. I was twenty, everyone was quite young. It was a nice environment there wasn't any bitchiness or back biting, which can be the way with a lot of women. There was a feeling of being part of an arty community."

Most of the decorators spent their time on the textured ware which was now dominating production. Anne Lewis was the only person allowed to do the 'ashtrays'. Those and the mugs were the only pieces of glazed ware left. Ruth remembers Anne working there,

"She was top dog decorator at that time. The longer you had been there, there was no official head decorator but it was just taken for granted who was top."

This first wave of employment in 1971 also marked the return of Roland Bence who had come back from Gloucestershire,

"We missed Cornwall badly so I bought a house in Penzance and I went and saw Leslie and apologised for my behaviour. He sat there at his desk and said 'look it's only because we are selling lots that we'll take you back'. So I was taken back under a cloud. And I did promise him that I could more or less double the output which is what I did."

"Being creative isn't the be all and end all. Being good at business is a pretty important thing."
John Bedding

Leslie was probably pretty relieved to see him. Here was someone who was skilled and could help with the mould-making, take some of the weight off. Ian Draper too was probably glad to see him, he was looking to move on and Roland's sudden appearance allowed him to leave without causing any problems.

During his time in Gloucestershire, Roland had been working at a large industrial pottery at Prinknash Abbey. Whilst there he observed processes and techniques which would allow him to fulfil his promise to double production. He revolutionised working practice.

Troika had always had difficulty drying out the moulds which would become saturated during slip casting. They had built shelves on top of the kilns in order to encourage the moulds to dry; these were lined with asbestos sheets. Roland now built proper drying cupboards which meant a mould could return to production in less time.

When a mould is filled with liquid clay it becomes very heavy and when emptied it has to be done smoothly so that the same volume of air enters the mould as slip comes out. This is to prevent a vacuum forming which would pull the clay away from the side of the mould and cause a shape to collapse. Roland installed casting benches with a lip to rest the moulds on and a smooth, sloped Formica surface that allowed the excess slip to run off into a gulley at the bottom. Three or four moulds could be lined up at an angle and would gradually empty themselves. More than one mould could be emptied at one time and it meant that the casters were free to do other jobs. The run off slip could be reused. These benches were much easier to clean and so provided a huge saving in time and materials. As it was physically possible to empty the moulds by resting them on the bench rather than having to hold them, larger pieces could be attempted.

The most important process that Roland developed was to do with sand. When Troika was based in St Ives sand would be painted onto the master block to provide the texture. From this block a textured mould was made. But through repeated castings the clay would quickly wear down the textured mould, which would soon become lumpy and eventually turn completely smooth and unusable. Another issue with the mould being textured was that it would inevitably leave a smooth line down the side of a pot where the two pieces of the mould had been placed together. During the fettling process, they would try to texture the smooth line. When this problem first became apparent in St Ives they scratched the surface with a knife, then later with sand paper.

Neither process ever looked consistent with the texture of the mould, so a visible line remained. They began to texture some pieces by painting a mixture of sand and slip onto the surface after they had been cast, rather than have them come out of a textured mould. This developed from the 'wheel vases' where the front would stay rough but the sides would quickly smooth out. This technique was extended to the cylinders where they could be spun on a wheel to paint the sand on.

Part of the reason that this process had not been fully developed and extended across the range was due to the type of sand they were using. Naturally, they had been getting sand from the beach but this had a high salt content. So when the pot was fired the sand would explode off in the kiln leaving holes. Roland discovered by experimentation that using sand meant for the floor of a budgie cage prevented this. It was finer in grain, would take the pigment when decorated and had no impurities. This had all happened in St Ives but when Roland returned to Troika he encouraged the painting of sand on all pieces. It was much quicker to paint on a mixture of sand and slip during the fettling processes than to fix up a semi-textured pot. It was also much easier to design a smooth master shape which would be textured afterwards.

This not only sped up production of what was now predominantly textured ware but also meant that the texturing became much more uniform, giving a higher quality finish. A feature of the Newlyn pieces is this uniformity of texture, whereas the pieces produced in St Ives are much rougher and often lumpy. As an interesting historical note this is the exact opposite trend to that described in previous studies of Troika.

Roland appreciated the potential for creativity in Troika's production techniques,
    "Something like that develops itself and a creative person will find a way. That's what is lovely about pottery, I actually prefer this kind of pottery to thrown pottery because you have to adapt. You can make anything, any shape, you are not restricted. I can emulate thrown stuff quite easily. At the end of the day I can change it."

Making pieces of Troika was a delicate process, as care had to be taken when filling the mould with clay to get an even cast without bubbles or lines. Much effort was taken during the fettling process to maintain the features and dynamics of the original design. Roland recalls the attention to detail which helps make the pieces still attractive today,
    "When you're putting plaster onto clay what happens is that air gets trapped and you end with a little bubble so you have to cut that out. That's done when they're wet or when they're

"[Leslie] got on well with the staff; he got on well with everybody... Leslie handled everybody much better than I did. He was much more laid back about it. I could get up tight about it."

Benny Sirota

dry and fettled. And they get bigger and bigger and bigger so that's what spoils the design on them, that's what you have to be on top of. You had to shake the mould. When you started you had to make sure you had enough clay in the bucket to fill the mould or you would get a line, a lot of potters make that mistake, you can see it in a lot of shapes. So when we had big wheels you had buckets full of clay, they were really heavy."

Due to the increased workload and the move, Troika had not brought out any new shapes since the Heal's exhibition. There was a plethora of new designs but no new shapes. As Troika settled into its new premises there was an influx of new shapes. There were many one-off experiments with new glazed pieces but these never entered full production, they mainly exist due to Leslie's personal preference for them.

The textured 'coffin vase' was the first new piece to establish itself. It wasn't immediately popular in the factory or with shopkeepers but it sold in huge quantities and attitudes began to change. It was named by the decorators and although the shape suggests its name, the name only stuck due to its initial unpopularity.

A tall piece of sculpture called 'the pillar' was made. It balanced wickedly on a tiny diamond-shaped base, as if waiting for the right moment to fall over. However, due to its clever weighting it was remarkably stable in real life. Leslie was seeing how far he could push the medium, how high could he build and how extravagant the point of balance could be.

It was only natural that the pieces would get larger now that there was more room to manoeuvre. Right from the beginning, pieces of Troika were often designed to interlock in the kiln. This would maximise the output of

'Mask', showing 'Aztec' front and 'Paul Klee' rear

> *"I think Leslie was having a bit of fun. We both liked Paul Klee, if you notice one side is real Paul Klee and the other side is Aztec."*
>
> Benny Sirota

each firing. The top of the new kiln had a large arch on it so 'large wheel vases' were made to follow the arc of the roof. The 'double base vase' and the 'large cylinder vase' increased in prominence now more could be made.

A more stable shape that emerged was the 'anvil'. However, the piece does not seem to identify with its name. It has none of the heaviness or resilience of an anvil. Like many artists Leslie was obsessed by the feminine form and it regularly featured in his work. This shape instead seems to resemble a tight corset. The feminine curves of hips and bust are proud yet fragile. The clay was thin due to the deftness of the casting and the piece feels light. This deft casting accentuates its fragility and a piece that could have been clumsy appears to float.

The fourth piece to appear soon after they moved to Newlyn was the 'mask'. Like the anvil, in real life it is lightweight and attractive. Not as large and frightening as it can often appear in photographs.

The 'mask' interestingly began as a joke. It was often observed that Troika looked quite Aztec so Leslie thought he would make something humorously representative. It had also been noted that certain shapes in his work looked like faces. So on one side of this piece was a face based upon an Aztec mask and on the other was an abstracted set of geometric figures, also presented as a face. In this light the mask became a clever piece of artistic instruction, showing the links between ancient history and modern art. Benny comments,

"I think Leslie was having a bit of fun. We both liked Paul Klee, if you notice one side is real Paul Klee and the other side is Aztec."

Judith remembers that Leslie was never truly satisfied with the mask, probably because the link to another artist was so strong.

The decoration on the new sculptural ware was produced through Troika's standard colour palette. The decorators had some flexibility in that they could layer colours to alter their tone but this was limited. Troika never developed its palette after this point largely due to Benny's increased separation from the production. Leslie was not so interested in the colours; he was interested in the shapes, in sculpture. The colours were now solely there to accentuate these forms but it would be entirely up to the decorators which elements were to be given primacy.

This new textured range became Troika's iconic line. Sculptural Troika pieces are without precedent because they were created as a direct result of the decisions and experiences which are Troika's personal history, rather than emerging from an historical movement. This makes them very difficult to categorise or understand. Celebrated local potter, Alan Brough described them as, "Very original, there was no influence or mentor. Troika was Troika. People have tried to copy it since. It wasn't historically viable to the intellectuals. Leslie was a modernist."

As a modernist and a sculptor Leslie did not follow the intellectual process that had brought pottery to its contemporary form, as Alan describes,

"Where they got the message wrong is that Bernard Leach said that a simplest bit of natural dirty clay can be made very beautiful if you put certain glazes on it and make it highly usable. Leach was highly visual. How something looks completely different if you use different clays. I don't think Leslie was interested in using different clays."

However, Benny was familiar with this concept and indeed admired it, which is why Troika's earlier pieces reflect an understanding of utility and craft. Benny would continue to explore these ideas in his own work.

Large 'cuboid' vase –
Designed by Leslie Illsley,
decorated by Anne Lewis,
c. 1972

Chapter Eleven

"As long as the pattern was geometric, you couldn't do flowers, nothing like that, but you could do what you like."

– Avril Bennett

Each lunchtime Leslie, and Benny if he wasn't working the shop, would disappear to the Swordfish. A tradition that had begun in St Ives. They chatted with the locals and the fisherman and it was here that they met local potter Alan Brough.

The drinking soon got heavier and Benny began to get fed up. Too many lively debates turned into heated arguments and the afternoons were getting harder and harder to work through. Benny remembers,

"Alan Brough was our drinking partner, but because he was a one-man band he had to get back... There was too much drinking in Newlyn. I just couldn't take it. It went on far too long, leaving everyone working at Troika and we were there with these fishermen and boy could they drink!"

Benny had an escape route. He was running the shop in St Ives and it was thriving. This arrangement was ideal as it allowed Troika to maintain a public face and to retain a base in St Ives, where the large tourist market was located. People associated St Ives with art and were fascinated by Troika's unusual designs. For Benny it also allowed him to be where he wanted to be. In the summer he would travel back and forth from St Ives to Newlyn most days of the week. When they closed the shop through winter Benny would return to Newlyn full time.

It is interesting that Benny and Judith continually refer to the place in St Ives as a shop. This moniker tallies with Troika's working ethic because in reality the shop was a gallery. Not many owners of similar establishments on Fore Street, or any number of quirky back alleys, call their 'bespoke art spaces' shops.

Nevertheless, in the shop they not only sold Troika pieces but a host of other high quality local artwork. Benny instigated the clever tactic of using Troika's purchasing power to give them an exclusive stock. This generated sales in the summer and it helped the local potters to make money during the winter. He recalls,

"It was mostly Troika but I would be buying stock all year round. We supported local potters and we would buy off them. We had the money from the sales of Troika so we would buy off them in the winter when they had nothing else to do. We bought Alan Brough's stuff, Anthony Richards. I would go round to each pottery and buy 500 quids worth of their stuff and stockpile."

Small 'wheel vase', c. 1975

Troika had set itself up from the beginning to be able to cope with the slump in local trade by going to London. Now they were able to help other local artists survive by buying up what often amounted to their entire winter's production, then sell it in the summer. Other shops across Cornwall were starting to do the same with Troika. Shop owners would come and make an order in the winter knowing that if they left it too late they would not be able to get any stock. Troika was selling out fast.

The shop also provided more jobs for the local people. Sarah Watson was their shop assistant in the summer of 1971. She was given one of the original cast apples by Benny as a present. She remembers that, "At the time it was new and different, it was that thing that people were looking for." Sarah spent the summer of '71 and '72 working there and then left to work in the New Craftsman Gallery. Benny then employed his partner Jacqui Jones to work with him, they subsequently married. Jacqui remembers the excitement in the shop,

"I worked in the shop in St Ives and I watched people coming in and making choices and going out, they weren't arty types, they were ordinary people, but they had critical discussions about the shapes, the styles, the colours."

Benny also remembers the reaction the pieces had,

"You had people coming in, real holidaymakers who would pick up a little pot of Troika, a little 'cube' and actually fondle it as if they were buying a bit of art, which they were."

Roland agreed that there was an intention to make art,

"They were made sculpturally. That was the idea, mass produced sculpture. A lot of our stuff wasn't utility it was huge great square things."

Judith claims it was Leslie's intention to spread art throughout the country,

"Those relief's on those pots were like his paintings, he wanted everybody, everybody please note, not just somebody, to own a piece of abstract art without them realising it."

Roland told us how important the pricing of pieces of Troika was in achieving this,

"It was all on price. I mean the 'cubes' were about 3 quid each. You could buy a 'wheel' pot for about two pound fifty. It was mad. Great big 'cylinders' for about a tenner. They were practical prices. I think it was probably Benny, he did most of the selling."

Troika had become Leslie's way of exposing ordinary people to abstract art. He was presenting the same abstract ideas that were present in his painting on the sides of the textured piece but unlike 'Sculptures for Living' he wasn't chasing an exclusive audience. However, in order to persuade the buying public to purchase a potentially useless piece of abstract art, an element of utility had to remain in most shapes. Judith raises the importance of use to the ordinary people who bought Troika,

"It wasn't just a painting it was a functional object, although people didn't often know what to do with it. I mean it was obviously a vase or a receptacle of some kind but you had to suggest a use for it, you could put pencils in it, or even turn it upside down."

Slip casting meant it was easy to retain a salutary element of practicality in their sculpture and so they were able to sell them. It is the hole in the top that makes it a vase, without it it is a totem. The hole in the top does not impede upon the sculptural form. It barely even suggests a function, so fundamentally it all came down to the name. Which is why to this day Troika pieces often have a descriptive noun after them such as 'vase' or 'jar' or 'pot'.

In order not to confuse or dilute the vision, it was only the Troika shapes that had a flat surface which could be used as a 'canvas', that exhibit reliefs. These ideas were never applied to generic, utilitarian shapes like the 'cylinders' or 'drum bowls'.

As in their original little showroom at Wheal Dream, the shop on Fore Street was attracting customers who may not ordinarily have been thinking about buying art. Troika was at the beginnings of what is now known as the democratisation of art. They, as practitioners, had already benefited from the idea by using clay as a readily available, relatively cheap material. Now they contributed toward the idea that everyone should be able to afford to surround themselves with art.

"You had people coming in, real holidaymakers who would pick up a little pot of Troika, a little 'cube' and actually fondle it as if they were buying a bit of art, which they were."

Benny Sirota

The democratisation of art can be seen to have roots in the block printing of seventeenth century Japan. This method was quickly embraced by artists to produce cheap art prints and books which could be more widely distributed. It meant the notion that art had to be a unique piece of work was challenged. Each picture was part of a print run. The art only existed once ink was applied to each of the separate blocks that held an element of the final image and they all were pressed onto paper. It is the resulting picture not the blocks which constitutes the art. The most famous work produced in this method is The Great Wave off Kanagawa by Hokusai.

This method of producing art is similar to Troika's production technique where the sculpted master block was cast. A piece of Troika is the resulting sculpture not the master block. The art emerged every time a cast was taken. Both techniques allow a singular vision to be disseminated to everybody and not just be owned by one person.

Through the sixties and the seventies popular culture rose to produce its own art for the enjoyment of everyone. This was often mass produced as the factory was reclaimed for the benefit of the general population. This reclamation had already been physically achieved by cultural movements of the early twentieth century such as Socialism, the Bauhaus and Constructivism. These movements inspired many artists of the sixties and seventies. Across the Atlantic in America, Andy Warhol even called his studio 'The Factory' and used printing and photography to disseminate large runs of a single, unique image.

The shop in St Ives helped realise one of Troika's dreams and shows why the Newlyn era was so important. With the new large factory Troika was able to produce enough pieces to reach a huge number of people. The art scene of St Ives may have seeded Troika but it was the down to earth dreams of Newlyn which inspired them to reach as many people as they could. Far from the move to Newlyn marking the decline in Troika, as has sometimes been suggested, it marked the beginning of their legacy.

Troika did have a little showroom in Newlyn which is where Leslie got a chance to have a go at selling, although for him it was more about interacting with people. Judith recalls,

"Leslie loved it, the people coming in. He was in his element because he was a very sociable person. I mean he'd talk to anybody. He'd spend a lot of time with them explaining what you could do with all of his different pots. He'd spend ages and ages with them. If they showed some interest he would take them through the whole process."

Leslie may have tried selling but he never took it seriously. Maybe he thought it was arrogant to force his work on people. Maybe he gained no satisfaction from the planning of a long-term strategy, the high of a sale soon wearing off. Maybe in truth it is difficult and requires a certain skill and personality. It is to Benny's credit that he was able to generate so many sales and actualise Troika's vision.

In the early seventies Benny was chasing sales hard in order to drive the expansion. He teamed up with Celtic Pottery which was run by the excellent businesswoman Maggie Fisher. Together they went up to the Torquay Trade Fair, held each year at the Palace Hotel. This was where all the local buyers would go to get stock. Benny managed to sell out an entire year's production in two days. Traders were supposed to stay for the full five days of the show so Maggie made a cardboard cut-out of Benny as his work there was done,

"I couldn't take any more. So because you weren't allowed to leave she put a little cut-out. Taking the piss."

The market was won over and Troika began to sell along the whole of the south coast, to a single shop in every town. Benny made it look easy. But this success illustrates the extent to which Troika not only joined the local fraternity but dominated. Alan remembers,

"I mean Tremaen and Celtic used to sell a lot but Troika made them look stupid. The businessmen in Newlyn would think they were all arty-farty... They couldn't understand how Troika was making so much money. They always wondered why the pots had gone so well. But Troika was very exciting to the public. They spent their money on it and people, even in those days, were very careful how they spent their holiday money."

Chapter Twelve

"Leslie was a really talented man. He taught me to develop my ideas, my techniques."

– Roland Bence

In 1973 the coal miners' disputes combined with the global oil crisis brought political and economic turmoil. This led to the introduction of the three day week in January 1974. Troika ignored Edward Heath's 'three day week order' and continued to work with the lights off, effectively breaking the law. None of the staff minded because they were still getting paid.

As the pressure on the economy mounted, for a brief moment Troika seemed under some financial pressure. A piece-rate was introduced to ensure the decorators were working to a maximum.

This draconian measure did not have the intended effect and was soon abandoned when they lost too many good decorators. The staff were motivated to work hard at Troika for the pride of creating pieces of art, however long this took, not to just churn out objects to make money. Roland remembers,

"We went through a period of them doing piece-work, really dodgy at one time, they had to start earning their money and they only got paid for what they did. It got really tight and a couple of girls left then because they were under pressure to produce enough to make a living."

Roland's improvements in practice and Benny's efforts in generating sales had been effective despite the worsening economic times. Troika recovered from this blip and continued to increase production. Roland remembers,

"When it was really busy we'd be firing kilns in quick succession. For a bisque firing you had to fire it for three hours with the bung wide open and bring it up slowly. The bung is the air vent at the back that lets the heat flow through, so things dry out before you shut it all in to get really hot. Timing all that was critical. Sometimes we knew we had to fire the kiln the next day so we were cracking it when it was red hot to let it cool down really quick. I've got asbestos hands from emptying the kilns; I can carry anything hot simply from getting hot pots out of the kiln."

A new group of decorators were employed to replace those that had left, taking the average number of employees up to 9. The new intake included Penny Broadribb and Avril Pellow. Penny was fed up with working at an advertising agency in London and came to Cornwall for a new life. She found a caravan out in the pristine wilderness of Lamorna and a job at a Warren's Bakery. She soon traded this in for the more preferable working environment of Troika, although the pay was little better.

As in St Ives, the stories from the decorators in Newlyn followed the same inexorable pattern. Troika was a lifeline, a real alternative to regular life. Avril Pellow, who became Bennett, was to become one of Troika's longest serving and most respected decorators. Avril was one of the few decorators who joined Troika later in life. She remembers how Troika inspired her to follow an artistic pathway,

"Fortunately I had some of the artistic bent in me and thank goodness. It was a lifeline for me. I don't know what I would have done...I was working in a shoe shop. They would very rarely advertise these sorts of jobs; you wonder how to get in through the door."

Avril was different to most of the decorators, who normally began working Troika when very young. There were at least two factors to this. One was that Leslie hated getting old so surrounded himself by young people. The other was that younger staff were paid less. For most of the younger people joining Troika, it was their first real job and as they had few outgoings, the wages were sufficient. However, once trained, they were on a full wage with no opportunity to increase it. Even the role of the Head Decorator was only a title of respect, it didn't come with an increase in wage. Therefore, decorators were forced to look elsewhere for a career path as their responsibilities, as well as their ambition, grew. This often meant leaving art behind as a source of income. Penny Broadribb lasted for four years at Troika before deciding it was time to move on to different things as she explains,

"It was more than a job because it was creative. I've worked as a waitress and all sorts of things, and this was much more satisfying. In the last year I think I got fed up of it. These Manpower schemes were coming in where the government would pay you to go on a training course which is what I did. I went to go on a secretarial course. It meant I could move on."

With all these young people together, the atmosphere at Troika was much more relaxed than in any office. Roland remembers the things that happened especially when Leslie was absent,

"Crazy things like clay fights, mad stuff that everyone does – mucking around sitting around for hours talking rubbish, smoking. Don was a smoker so we'd sit outside and a couple of the girls would join in."

This atmosphere may have helped the workers deal with the often difficult working environment. Troika had embraced industrial processes and with these came a potentially dangerous mix of dust, heat and heavy metals. Attitudes were different in the seventies and there was little consideration given to health and safety. Masks were never worn, manganese glaze was mixed by hand, asbestos was used to line the drying-shelves on top of the kilns and sometimes exploded due to the intense heat, spraying a fine mist of toxic particles throughout the building. If staff left after a few months it was normally because they couldn't cope with these industrial conditions, the dust and the sickly smell of paraffin and wax.

Avril recalls how staff had to keep their wits about them and look after themselves,

"I do remember in hot weather the upstairs doors were open, the loading bay doors, there was a ten foot drop, it would have been easy to fall out but nobody did. There was no sign you just had to be careful... We had a pan on top of a Bunsen burner with melted candles in paraffin! (This was to keep the wax fluid so it could be painted onto the pieces) For the wax resist work. I remember one Saturday, mine caught fire and I ran to the sink with it and it went all over my hands but it's surprising you don't even notice the pain. Health and safety wouldn't allow you to do it now but it worked fine then."

Roland remembers that he almost got electrocuted performing repairs to a kiln,

"I was nearly killed. In the back of the kilns there were lots of electrical elements to heat it. They were wired in series in blocks of six. If one element went the whole block would go and the kiln would struggle to reach temperature. So what we would do is take the back off, take a copper wire and miss that element out. All the controls were upstairs so I'd be downstairs putting the wire on and shouting upstairs to Don to turn the kiln on and off. But he was boiling a kettle and I thought he shouted "it's off", but he actually shouted "what". And I just caught hold of it. 1500V (*laughs*) it blew me across the floor. Unbelievable. My hair stood out, I was burnt."

These situations could not continue forever and Roland explains how health and safety finally had to become a serious consideration,

"We got them to wear face masks in the end. Sometimes you would go upstairs when a kiln was firing, when we had both big kilns firing and it, the air, would be blue. I mean Benny never wore a face mask when he was glazing with lead tin glaze. He would be covered from head to toe in glaze dust. You fill the pot up and then you tip it out and it's all round the edge so you had to brush it off. It goes on as a liquid but turns to powder and you'd brush it off. In St Ives there was a window on the side behind where Stella was sitting decorating, the glass had gone frosted from the chemicals in the firings. It was clear and it went frosted, when I arrived it was kind of opaque and by the time I left it was pitted with frost."

Downstairs, where the casting and fettling was a constant process, Roland had been making the copies of the moulds. It was only in the evening that he was able to let his creative side

"Crazy things like clay fights, mad stuff that everyone does – mucking around sitting around for hours talking rubbish, smoking. Don was a smoker so we'd sit outside and a couple of the girls would join in."

Roland Bence

Sections of the mould for the 'Venetian blind' lamp

take over. He had his own set of keys and often stayed late into the night listening to jazz whilst making his own plaques and pots, which he signed RGB. A lot of these went to America and made him a good income on the side.

Leslie had been taking note of Roland's own artistic flair and real interest in the processes of creation. It was suggested that Roland might want to start actually creating some master moulds, with his own designs on. This was unprecedented; Leslie was very precious about Troika's identity. Since Benny stopped contributing to the range with thrown ware he had never allowed anyone to get this close and had never allowed anyone else to create moulded work. Leslie began to teach Roland about his process.

Leslie was an abstract artist who began with the assumption that shape, not the natural world, was one of the essential characteristics of art. He was impressed by Paul Klee's idea that drawing was like "taking a line for a walk". He would often be playing with different substances, drawing his finger through spilt beer on a table or dust on a mirror. The shapes that emerged fascinated him and influenced the shapes on the pieces. He was rarely interested in straight lines, preferring to interrupt any definite stroke by using an uneven tool, such as ship rivets or chicken bones.

Roland tries to explain Leslie's practice,

"Not many people knew what his shapes meant. But they had a specific meaning. He was very precious over his style…Some of them were quite sexually explicit which you wouldn't know unless you knew what they were, because they were quite abstract. Some of them had

"I started making moulds and it took a long time for me to get to a standard that he would accept… I had to adapt into doing stuff that he would say was Troika"

Roland Bence

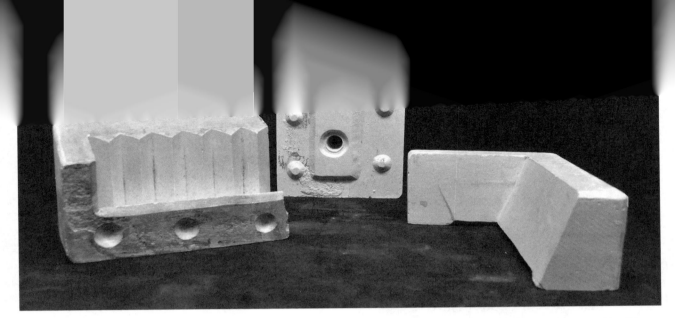

Sections of the mould for the 'Venetian blind' lamp

hidden messages in them, some of them had words in them – if you didn't know they were there you wouldn't see them.

A lot of shapes were influenced by the tools we used; some shapes were made with an old car valve just pushed into the clay. Other shapes are made with an old rivet, big ships' rivets of different sizes."

He encouraged Roland to express himself and draw influences not from nature but from symbols that he admired and to express them through abstract geometry. Roland remembers that Leslie expected a high standard of work,

"I started making moulds and it took a long time for me to get to a standard that he would accept. I was doing pretty wild stuff and he would say that's not Troika. It's either Troika or not Troika, so I had to adapt into doing stuff that he would say was Troika. I couldn't copy his style. I had to do my own style but it had to be Troika!"

Roland passed the test and his work began to be introduced into the Troika range. As he points out there is a distinct difference between his and Leslie's work,

"Where Leslie would more often cut into the clay, I would build up. So we had quite defined, quite different ways of using that basic shape. My designs haven't got much drawing in. That's probably because I wasn't allowed to but probably because I couldn't do it as well as Leslie. But I could still make nice shapes."

It was not only that Roland would build up the clay more. Roland's designs relied heavily on reflectional, or mirror, symmetry and used bold, definite lines where the patterns in the clay were powerfully segmented and regimented. A lot of this was probably to do with the fact that Roland was having to work to a remit and all this without copying Leslie. Roland started incorporating real world symbols into his designs. Fragments of his observed life integrated into a piece of Troika. Some were taken directly from company logos others had a spiritual underpinning,

"A lot of my designs were bold, very different from the things Leslie did. I am influenced by American Indian symbols. The Guinness sign is mine, there's a front view of a VW somewhere. An eclipse, the sun sign, the stairway to

Above:
'Helmet' sculpture

Opposite:
'Venetian blind' lamp

heaven, two people in a parachute, silly things like that. The swirl, I was very proud of that one."

The simplicity and direct communication of Roland's designs appealed to the shop-keepers and the public and they started to sell as well as Troika ever had. They provided an interesting counterpoint to Leslie's work and offered an alternative perspective from which to appreciate the Troika shapes.

Roland had now effectively served his second apprenticeship and had become a fully qualified member of Troika. He had experience in running every facet of the business and could generate new work.

Leslie's experiments with glazed ware continued and around 1974 Leslie made the 'helmet'. It was partly inspired by an interest with Roman armour and partly by a short obsession with a milliner's hat block, used for stretching hats that lived on a shelf at Leslie's house. The helmet began as a sculpture that Leslie made from plaster which he then cast in two pieces; these were held together with slip. The shape of the helmet was a complex arrangement of layered cylinders. As if an egg had been grabbed by a giant with powerful hands and twisted.

In it can be seen the influence of Leslie's youthful admiration of Henry Moore. Roland used to joke how 'Moore-ish' Troika was, although Moore's influence was only really tangible in the 'helmet'. Although sold as a piece of pure sculpture it was often included in Troika's range in the guise of a lamp base. There was a conscious decision to once more try and extend Troika's sculptural scope and to use multiple moulds to make a single object. The 'Venetian blind' lamp also appeared at around this time.

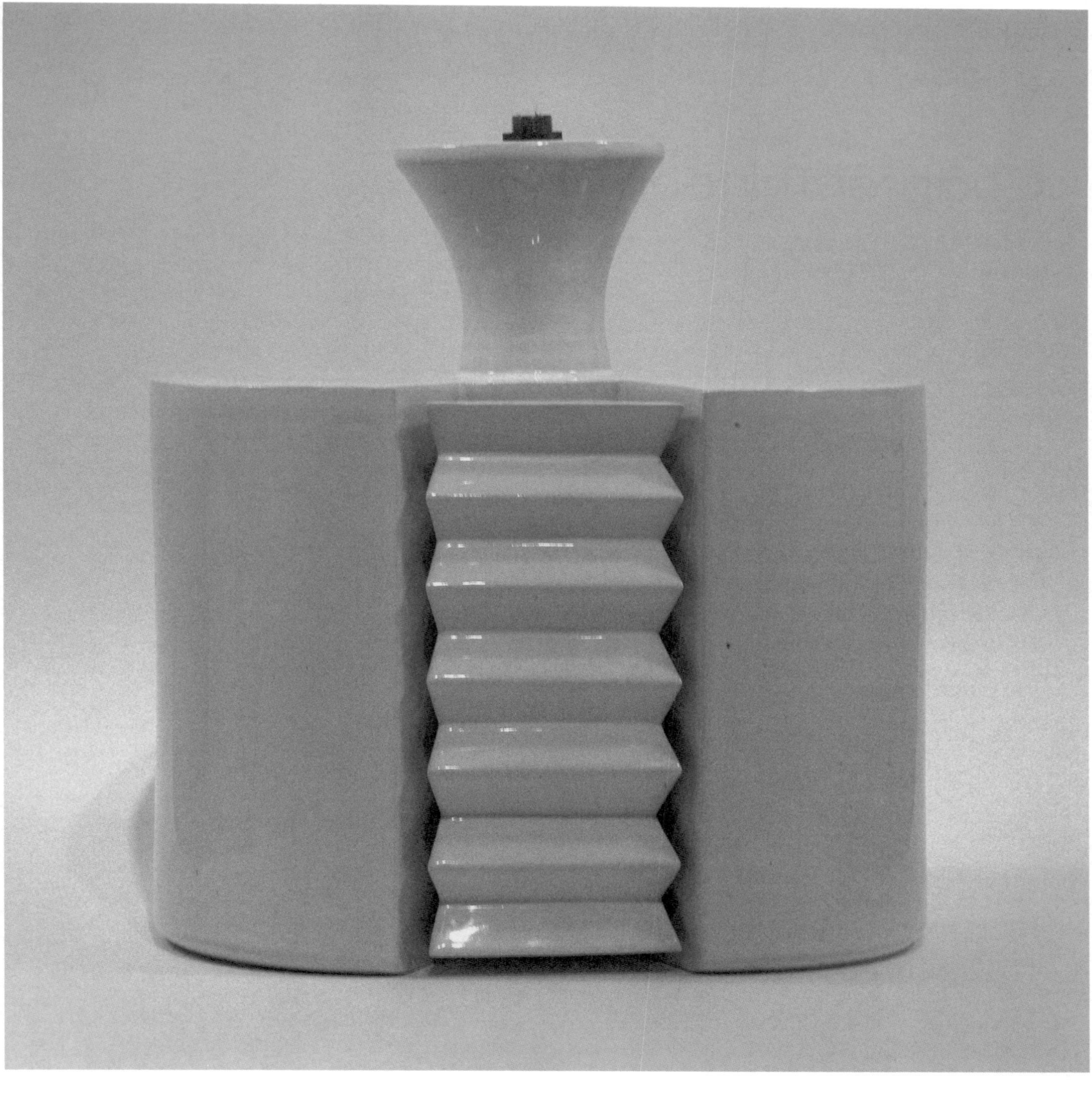

Chapter Thirteen

"He told me that he had just spent the afternoon talking to the fishermen about Cezanne and Klee. Why? Leslie wanted to be an artist but he wanted to be a working man too, he needed that validation."

– Bryan Illsley

In 1974, Troika sold the house the company had bought in Penzance and immediately bought their shop in St Ives with the flat above it. It meant that as the money had been reinvested straight away, they avoided Capital Gains Tax. This was known as 'bed and breakfasting'. Then Benny and Leslie opened another new shop in Newlyn. It was right by the Swordfish.

Margaret Gunn, a local businesswoman, joined them as an investor and became the manager. Margaret kept a bottle of wine under the counter and Leslie would often stop off to have a chat. The shop in Newlyn lasted for one summer. They had only agreed a short-term lease with the landlord who, when he saw that it was doing well, increased the rent thereby making further investment uneconomic.

When the shop closed in Newlyn Benny was running out of reasons to come to Newlyn. He was forging a whole life for himself in St Ives. He had the shop and had just become a landlord. One of their tenants in the flat was Molly Parkin, the designer and fashion magazine editor. Benny and Jacqui were planning a family and in June of 1974 Sophie was born. Benny used his spare time to follow other interests. His interest in classical music meant that he helped to found the St Ives September Festival. He also furthered his aspirations as a studio potter.

When Troika first moved to Newlyn, Benny would be at Fradgan Place a lot, especially in the winter when the shop in St Ives was shut. He was in the office, dealing with invoices and packing up the orders. He used his background in lithographic printing to develop the stylish Troika typeface, it was used as a header on all their correspondence and marketing material. All the pieces for the shops would be packed into bulging cardboard boxes with Troika on the side. They had a binding machine to hold the boxes together. At first Troika would pack their pots with newspaper but as Judith puts it "the posh shops complained so they changed to wood wool."

Benny remembers, "At the beginning I spent a lot of time at Newlyn, I was back and forth. I can't really remember. I must have been there for at least the first three or four years."

By 1975 Benny was being slowly pushed out of Fradgan Place by Leslie who had taken over every aspect of production. When the 'mugs' were removed from the range in the mid seventies, not a single piece that had originally been thrown remained. The wheel had stayed behind in St Ives so no new thrown pieces could be added to the range, casting was ubiquitous. Roland was packing the kiln and when Don began to pack the boxes there was nothing left for Benny to do. Judith remembers,

"I know Leslie was very possessive about Newlyn, he didn't even want Benny there. I think Benny did feel that he was pushed out. I can understand that."

As Benny's role in production slowly disappeared, he spent less time at Fradgan Place and his absence began to be noticed by the decorators as Penny's comments suggest,

"Benny was there but never in the building. He would pop in from time to time. He was more of a sleeping partner wasn't he?"

Avril gives a clue that something may have been going on,

"Benny always was a chirpy fellow, we would see him now and again and then eventually he didn't come any more, it was quite strange. Something happened in 1975."

Physical distance had separated the two partners and now they were growing apart personally. The crack that had been slowly opening soon became a chasm. Roland remembers a particularly fateful day,

"Benny came down one day and there was nobody there. Don was there with two decorators and he wanted to know where everyone was. So he stormed into the Swordfish demanding... I never heard the full story but we didn't see Benny after that."

Leslie had begun to spend more time in the Swordfish and was relying on the others to keep production going. Newlyn had changed Leslie, his drinking had become obsessive. What was part of the fun of St Ives had become serious. Benny had had enough of drinking in general and didn't like being harangued by Leslie, so simply stayed away.

"It was difficult, Leslie drank. Just one over and that tipped him, not violent but he could talk. In the end we did just spread apart. In the end I was going to Newlyn less and less. My base was St Ives and Leslie's was Newlyn."

Benny had begun to wonder what exactly Leslie was doing at Newlyn other than watching the pieces leave the factory and then going to the pub. With Benny not in Newlyn, Leslie was starting to think exactly the same thing; that he was doing all the work, making all of the pieces, but taking the same money home. These little niggles became more pronounced as the alcohol enhanced the swing of Leslie's emotional pendulum. The partnership had changed. The meeting of minds and balance of identities had been evaporating.

Now they were barely even friends. Judith thinks,

"A partnership is like a marriage. It is difficult in a partnership, no one seems to be doing anything and so when one person does something they feel like they are doing it all."

The shop in Newlyn turned out to be the last new venture the partners took on together. Now separated Leslie and Benny hardly talked to each other. The business was running smoothly so there wasn't even the impetus of practical problems to spark a dialogue. When they did talk, it was on the phone and they often argued. These arguments never went anywhere because the business was making so much money without either of them having to do much.

To add to this, both men now had other partners to listen to their grumbles and provide a supporting shoulder. Leslie had Judith, Benny had Jacqui and a new baby. Each couple lived in a country house in a tiny hamlet, miles from each other. One family never visited the other. In the earlier years with less stable romances Leslie and Benny would have been able to rely on each other.

The lack of communication had caused resentment to build. Leslie retreated into himself because of his issues with Benny and did not see why he should put so much effort into the business any more. He ignored the potential of the 'helmet' and a new sculptural line and stopped making pieces altogether. Roland was left to look after the day to day running of the factory. By 1976 his responsibilities had grown considerably,

"I would always go down the bank and collect the money for the wages. I used to hate it. I used to go down the Swordfish and have a drink before I went because standing in the queue was a nightmare. The Newlyn snails they called us. We left a trail, there was white clay dust everywhere. You could tell where everyone had been, down to the fag shop, down to the corner shop to get sweets and stuff."

This had an unforeseen consequence for Leslie. Now that he had a wing man holding the fort, his lunch breaks in the pub slowly extended into the whole afternoon.

"There were occasions when I would finish a mould off. He would do one side and I'd do another because he didn't get back from the pub. That's literally how it happened. It had to be done while it was still workable. I think he became the boss who didn't have to be there."

His disappearance didn't happen overnight; Leslie gradually spent more and more time in the pub. It was not only Benny's absence but for Leslie, this was the first time in a long time he

"It was difficult, Leslie drank. Just one over and that tipped him, not violent but he could talk. In the end we did just spread apart. In the end I was going to Newlyn less and less. My base was St Ives and Leslie's was Newlyn."

Benny Sirota

felt that he didn't have to knuckle down. Whilst still in his twenties he had married, had two children and started a business. Now that it was successful he was enjoying some freedom. Judith remembers "a lot of craziness in Newlyn."

Roland was running everything so well that the workshop kept on producing even when Leslie wasn't there. He would often join Leslie and Alan down at the Swordfish at lunchtime, he remembers,

"The rows we used to have in the pub about art. And they weren't light-hearted they were really serious about what you could and you couldn't do. I'd go down there maybe half twelve, one o'clock for my lunch and we'd get into this row or get into a real heavy discussion about art or whatever and about quarter of an hour after I should have gone back Leslie would suddenly realise and remember that I worked for him and say 'hey you should be back, go on'. And I'd say 'You come with me then', then he'd say 'I run the show'. I'd take off then because it would be pointless and quite often I'd go from the back bar where Leslie drank to the front bar and he wouldn't know, so I'd be ripping it off as well."

A feedback loop was developing. The more time Leslie spent in the pub the more Roland began to develop new work. The more Roland took on, the less Leslie had to be up at Fradgan, the less he was there the more he drank. Leslie would often depart the pub for Alan Brough's pottery, in order to drink some whiskey. It became known as 'Alan's club'. Roland didn't notice that the fun was starting to turn into a problem,

"I just thought that Leslie wants to be the boss so he's just staying out of it and letting me run it."

Penny describes how it seemed to her,

"I think he was drunk most of the time to be honest. It was sad. He would go out at about eleven and come back in the afternoon drunk. We used to talk about it all the time. It was a big joke back then. We were quite flippant about it. 'Leslie's pissed again'. We were all a lot younger in those days, lifestyle catches up with you and you start taking things more seriously."

Leslie's absence meant that Roland's designs had become the dominant feature of Troika in the mid seventies. From 1975 onwards he started introducing new shapes. There were many that were tried and nearly made it; some became part of the range including 'the brick' and 'the globe'.

"I moulded a beach ball and then painted it with sand and slip. And I had developed that big round one and an urn type shape with handles, not many of them were made, a polo mint with a big circle and a triangular foot, quite a few of those were made. They were never

"There were occasions when I would finish a mould off. He would do one side and I'd do another because he didn't get back from the pub. That's literally how it happened. It had to be done while it was still workable. I think he became the boss who didn't have to be there."

Roland Bence

The 'Globe'

photographed, they were never established, yet they sold really well. We were making a lot
of them in the end."

The decorators preferred decorating the shapes without any surface motifs. The 'globe'
allowed them the most freedom of all and they thrived, especially Avril,

"Mostly the patterns were already on, because Roland and Leslie did most of the incised work
and we just coloured it in. It was just a matter of knowing what colours to put on because they
just looked all grey when they came out. It was a bit of a treat when we got to do a 'globe' or
something. I really felt that was part of me. The hardest was the 'globe', putting geometric on
that was not easy. It looked like lotus flowers, when you have the triangles coming up. I used the
edge of the sandpaper for a ruler. Sandpaper was very useful actually you could work over the
line in wax and then sandpaper it back. It was all done by eye. It was quite tricky to judge how
many of these triangles to put around, the 'globes' were quite big."

Selection of Troika pieces, including a large 'cylinder', which was cast from a drain-pipe.

During this fallow period Leslie made the 'hanging basket' as a reaction to Roland's 'globe'. He wanted to prove that he still could do it. It was essentially a practical item and not in any way as artistic as the 'helmet' or much of the rest of the Newlyn output. But if it was turned upside down it resembled a cap nut. An elongated hemisphere resting on an hexagonal base.

Roland recalls,

  "Leslie would come in at about 10am full of determination to make stuff and come half past ten he'd be gone. I knew where he was but he was out of my hair, I could carry on working. Then he'd come back at half past three in the afternoon, pissed as a rat and Judith would come and pick him up. Then I'd start to pack the place up and be off. He would have great spurts of conscience and make a new shape with the full intention of really knuckling down. You couldn't get away with just churning it out, you had to develop. I think I made about three pieces, totally my stuff, then he had a pang of conscience about it, came in and made the hanging basket. I think that was the last thing I saw him develop."

Now Roland was managing the business a lot of his surface designs had their basis in practicality. His use of distinct shapes meant they could be coloured in quickly. This would help the decorators produce as many as possible as it was obvious where to place the different colours.

Roland remembers that Leslie had still retained authority and the control of the wage book. Everyone still knew he was in charge, even if he wasn't there as much.

Louise Jinks decorating in Newlyn

"There was one seat that got the sun in the summer for an hour and a half and they would barter for that seat. I would be asked "can we have a long lunch break?" "Yes sit outside sun's shining. Get in half an hour late." That didn't happen if Leslie was around to keep it in order."

Leslie was relaxed most of the time but would let them know if he wasn't happy. He was forever concerned with the quality and expected a high standard wherever work was concerned.

"Sometimes we would get seconds. If there was a fingerprint it would be the end of the world. High standards. That's why it was successful."

Penny agrees with Roland,

"Leslie was very relaxed with us as long as the work went on. High standards, if it wasn't perfect it would go. That lamp is a second I don't know what's wrong with it [pointing to her own lamp], I think it's too light. If you missed any it would be rejected. He was always concerned."

Now that he had less to do, Leslie would often occupy himself with conversation. Roland remembers that often Leslie would come back from the pub, make himself a cup of coffee and start teasing the decorators. Trying to play the 'boss' character. He would try to instigate arguments and discussions. "I'd go up and say 'you're wasting their time Leslie. Leave them alone.'"

If a customer came into the showroom he would either embrace them or berate them depending on his mood. Above everything he was still proud of Troika.

   "He spent hours with people and if they liked the pots he would keep them there for ages, showing them all over the place. Then others he'd go 'bugger off I don't like you, I'm not selling that to you.' That was the booze talking most of the time, any other time he was great. He was a lovely man and he just had this thing about changing when he'd had a few drinks. I suppose that's what we do – we protect ourselves. He was an artist and that's the character of a creative eccentric. Some of them would get special treatment but if it was later in the afternoon they might actually get chucked out. 'Get out of my bloody workshop you fucking tourists', occasionally came out. Whatever took his fancy. He was quite a character." – Roland

Sales kept rising as the demand for Troika was never sated. As staff members left, new decorators were immediately employed including Louise Jinks,

"I just remember the list we had to get through, 3 trays of wheel pots, it was bonkers. When I started it was bedlam trying to get the work done, that was for Heal's"

By the end of the summer in 1977 the pressure and time constraints of running Troika's incessant production began to take their toll on Roland, like they had on Leslie before him. He was working too hard to concentrate on new designs and the pieces were in danger of becoming repetitive.

   "We worked with latex for a while to try and keep the texture. So we made quite a few pots from latex masters. But then the danger was that we would be pushing out the same thing. That was always a balance. I couldn't keep up with new designs because I was actually running the show. Quite often I had to do a lot of other work. Kiln packing, order packing, making sure that the decorators had stuff to decorate, teaching the girls how to glaze and trying to do my own stuff in there as well."

Roland was getting frustrated. He was left in charge but was never put in charge. Leslie wouldn't completely trust him to run the factory and would immediately usurp any authority Roland had when he came back from the pub.

Roland was virtually running the business and getting no credit. As in St Ives ten years earlier Leslie had promised him the world. The word partnership was often mentioned but always remained a dangling carrot. He began arguing with Leslie about the future but to little effect.

"I think he said to me if you develop ten pots and they are saleable and they sell well then you can justify that partnership and it was taken quite seriously. When I got right to the end I said well I've done this, I've done this, I've done this, I'm here all the time, it runs because I am here, why can't I have recognition in the partnership?"

Eventually, in late 1977, Roland threw his keys at Leslie and quit Troika for good.

"That's why I left I was absolutely making everything, making all the moulds, running the factory and getting no recognition whatsoever. I was falling out with Leslie a lot. I would be there from 6am, I'd get there really early to turn the kiln off, then I would make stuff. I had lost interest in the end. I was really struggling to be enthusiastic about it."

Roland never thought that Leslie saw him as different to the rest of the staff. Unbeknown to Roland, his name had been omitted from the wage book since 1973. This appears to offer some small token of recognition.

"I am really intrigued by this wage book. I am wondering if he had me down as a manager on a separate sheet. He never acknowledged that... I fell out with him, he didn't respect me but I had a real respect for him, no question, especially as an artist."

Chapter Fourteen

*"When the kiln timers broke down I used to
have to go in at two o'clock in the morning
and put them on, put the bung in. I worked all
sorts of weird hours in Newlyn."*

– Roland Bence

Julian Greenwood-Penny was employed in June 1977 as a young apprentice. He remembers first meeting Leslie.

"My first impression of him was sitting slightly troll-like behind his desk which was basically a plank of wood covered in drawings... Leslie was almost a cartoon. Because there was the perennial slightly bad hair cut, slightly longer hair at the back. It was never properly combed. He wore a jacket, a corduroy one and there was another one which was sort of almost wax melt, and jeans. I never saw him in a proper pair of trousers. You could almost draw him like that. I never saw him in a t-shirt always a shirt."

At first Julian mostly made the tea and fetched Leslie bottles of Haig whiskey from the local shop; which he soon refused to do. When Roland left, Leslie began Julian's education,

"Leslie had been lending me books to extend my education, Zola, a Leach Pottery book, a book of London after the blitz. All these photographs of bombed-out sites, he said 'I used to play on them as a kid'. Him and his brother Bryan had this tandem bicycle, running round London."

As he had done with Roland before, Leslie took a shine to this keen young man and found some inspiration through his presence, a chance to show off his skills again. For the last few years he had put art on the back burner and had been enjoying his freedom, or wasting his talents, whichever way you prefer to look at it.

Roland's absence set a new cycle in motion and forced Leslie to confront his inactivity. It forced him to come back into Fradgan Place to work because now there was no one else to do it.

Don had never really showed any interest in making moulds and was happy to remain fettling so Leslie started to develop Julian's skills. Leslie always liked to have an audience to show off his artistic prowess. Julian recalls,

"He recognised in me an odd talent and I recognised in him a great talent. He taught me how to make moulds. I would be trying to figure it out and Leslie would come over and say 'No! No! No!', he would flip it round and it worked."

It was an exciting place for a young man; art, booze, girls and the odd famous person popping by whom Leslie had met down the pub. Troika paid its staff on Thursdays and Thursdays was gig night at the local Winter Gardens in Penzance. A new era of punk was emerging and Penzance was actually on the gigging circuit. The Sex Pistols, The Police,

The Damned, Dexy's Midnight Runners all came and played. The hangover from the sixties had faded and now new attitudes and tastes were emerging, the country was in transition.

This period marks a period of artistic renaissance for Leslie and subsequently Troika. He was once more to be found with white dusty hands making new designs and master shapes upstairs in the plaster room, behind a plastic curtain, near the decorators.

The old boss was back; he had his family around him and began to cultivate this feeling. Judith began working there in 1979. She had a lot of tricks played on her as she was the boss's partner but gave as good as she got. Julian remembers,

"The day before she came, I am climbing about on the beams with this big spider, quite realistic and tied it up there with very fine wire. Judith was decorating and this spider came down very slowly and she freaked out. She retaliated the next day. Don, who she blamed for the incident opened his lunch box to find it filled with plastic flies. Next time there was a rash of those little things you step on and go bang. She gave as good as she got. Fair enough. Then the final thing was that Leslie walked out of the office stood on lots of them and went ballistic. 'This now stops!' It did, but it moved into different areas."

Jane Fitzgerald, remembers joining in and playing practical jokes on Leslie,

"I know he didn't forgive me once because I got a rubbery old man mask and his rain coat, I think he had just topped his coffee with whiskey and when he came in I made this noise like an old man and he nearly had a heart attack, he wasn't impressed. You see he always reminded me of my dad, he's the same temperament. Slightly grumpy sometimes but a really soft centre. You know, exactly as Leslie was."

Louise remembers his reaction,

"It really frightened the crap out of him. I can still hear the screams and then he really told her off... I think it was at the back end of a whole lot of practical jokes and then he really did have enough."

Troika had entered a new era. Fradgan Place started to become a genial place full of pranks and good feeling. Leslie now seemed to want to be much closer to those people who were important to him rather than the random people in the pub. There was even a Christmas staff party in the Swordfish, previously Leslie's personal province where he went to escape the workshop.

Leslie was beginning to spread his influence throughout the building again. He would always be around to negotiate about sick pay or holidays, or to help solve personal problems.

"[Leslie] really wanted other people to take chances with their lives. He helped people find their way."
Bryan Illsley

By this time Troika had begun to introduce a paid holiday in line with national expectations, although not law. Most people took a week's paid leave. Louise remembers Leslie drawing on their wage packets, "We used to have these silly little wage packets and he would write silly little things on them sometimes."

Julian remembers how Leslie dealt with a new piece of government legislation,
   "We had two toilets up behind the office, Leslie found legislation that he had to go and put male and female signs on them. So he found a nude photo of a woman and put it on one door, found a nude photograph of a man and put it on the other. These were taken off after it was found to be much simpler to put a leg of one of the 'legged cubes' up. He chopped off two legs fired them up, drilled a hole in the base of the leg and it was screwed to the door. One pointing out, and the other a cup. Very Troika."

In the background Leslie was having to deal with some serious issues. 1978 had been quite a turbulent year for Troika. Roland had left and Heal's began to reduce their orders. Heal's had appointed a new director and the company was trying to cope with the difficult economic climate. The 'ceramics' department had changed its name to the less evocative 'china'. They began to stock cheap transfer-printed home-ware and the decision was made to stop supporting studio pottery, amongst which they counted Troika. Modern materials were taking over as tastes began to change. In their catalogue cheaper moulded plastics began to appear where ceramics had once been.

Other national and local sales were still strong but the loss of the Heal's contract made Benny consider his future. He was spending a lot of time away from the shop to concentrate on his new ventures as he explained,
   "I worked in the shop and then I got someone else to work in the shop and opened up another business, a restaurant, 'Benny's Bistro', in 1978. I got into a partnership with Eddie Norman of Pegotty's, the local club. It never took off it was too early. Today it would be the biggest gold mine."

The restaurant was not the huge success it was hoped. Leslie didn't react well to Benny's new business venture as Jacqui points out, "There was a lot of enmity, strong feelings about Benny getting into another business because he was slowly pulling out."

Judith thought that Leslie felt abandoned.

"Leslie was really upset, they had always done things together and he was in business with Leslie and was being paid by Troika to run the shop. Benny was being paid to run the shop and he wasn't doing that."

Benny's family was growing, in the September of '79 his son Theo was born. So Benny, actively looking for other avenues of income, took his craft pottery aspirations a step further. He set up a new pottery in his house and decided to create his own pieces.

"I had this huge gas kiln built at Giew House. I got it from a mate of mine who I played snooker with, fortunately he had a bakery. He was buying a new kiln and he gave me the old burners and all the bricks. I began making these pots, totally different to Troika and John Bedding came and did a lot of throwing for me. I was designing them and throwing myself but I couldn't throw nearly as fast as him. I put the pots I made into the shops. I wasn't wholesaling, just the odd few bits, domestic ware. Cider pots and things like that"

Through the years Benny's side projects had been a source of irritation to Leslie. He had been solely occupied with Troika and had never spent time pursuing other endeavours. He felt tied to the factory and resented Benny's freedom. Although Leslie had slowly pushed Benny out of the production of Troika, they were still earning an equal amount of money from the business. Now that these side projects had become commercial endeavours they became more than niggles, they were competition. The tension had built up and with these latest escapades, exploded. Benny and Leslie began having major arguments about money. Louise gives an account of the mood,

"People were anxious that they were going to have a ding-dong and it was going to be really scary, just remember feeling a little agitated and like oh crumbs, Benny's coming"

Julian tells how a cloud fell over Leslie and Fradgan Place whenever the partnership was mentioned,

"Benny was an absent figure. He would come over and there would be rows in the office between him and Leslie, the door was closed but you could have heard them in the Swordfish. Afterwards Leslie's equilibrium went and all he could do was walk around with a dark cloud hanging over him for two days. So no he wasn't popular because of the aftermath of his visits. I can understand both points of view but it didn't make for a healthy working environment. The rows were about money."

Leslie's drinking got heavier to deal with the flood of emotions from the arguments. He had begun to realise that it had gone too far. Julian remembers witnessing an epiphany,

"Leslie drank but the lowest point I ever saw him, and it was our fault, was the Christmas '79. The decorators upstairs bought Leslie a bottle of Haig whiskey, unbeknown to Don and I downstairs who bought him half a bottle of Haig whiskey. I remember seeing him in his office staring at one and a half bottles of whiskey and I realised that he would have actually been happier if someone had painted him a Christmas card, bought him an interesting book, or done anything apart from pander to his vice."

"I think the paintings were the saving of him in many ways."
Julian Greenwood-Penny

Leslie realised that the best thing he could do was to be creative. His first love, sculpting, had become inseparable from Troika so now he turned to painting to assuage some of his personal demons, as he had done in the past. He had renewed his passion for painting and began allowing himself the necessary time and emotional commitment to fulfil that vocation. Rather than drinking in order to forget about the often heavy burden and responsibility of wasting his talent. It is telling that Roland did not know Leslie painted at all until he saw one of his paintings in an auction years after he had left Troika,

"I didn't realise that he was into his painting and I could suddenly see how it connected with Troika, how his drawings connected with Troika. He was an artist who was establishing in many ways. So the more he could produce the better."

Leslie began to exhibit his abstract paintings in the Orion gallery in Newlyn. He also began to chat about painting with Louise, who is now an established artist,

"I would put him as a real key person in my career really, because he was such a creative man and so enthusiastic and passionate about painting, I loved it, he would call me down for a painting chat when I was supposed to be working, and he would lend me books...because he was mad about Paul Klee, it was lovely, really generous. Klimt, Picasso, a big Beatles fan"

This encouragement was typical of Leslie. Bryan his brother gives us a real insight,

"Leslie had the gift of sympathy, not in a bullshit way but intuitively. He knew what people needed to hear, what they liked. He made all these people who came for a job believe they could do what he was asking of them, which was in fact highly skilled and very difficult. He really wanted other people to take chances with their lives. He helped people find their way. As children we were constantly told that we weren't worth a brass farthing and it was such a relief in later life to find out that this wasn't true. Leslie probably didn't want others to go through their lives thinking they weren't worth anything."

On Friday afternoons Leslie encouraged the staff to use the space for their own project. Jane remembers spending one Friday afternoon decorating mugs for her boyfriend Hugh, as it was his birthday,

"We used to finish early on a Friday. Finished at 12.30. But we could experiment in the afternoon. I had some mugs once and put 'to Hughy baby' on the bottom. I didn't put them in the kiln, Leslie did and he unpacked it and sent it off to Heal's. So someone had a set of 6 mugs with 'to Hughy baby' on the bottom."

Through painting, teaching and making moulds again Leslie began to consider the future of Troika. He could feel the partnership with Benny disintegrating and realised that there had been little artistic progression for the last five years. It was all in danger of collapsing, just at the moment when he was beginning to see its worth. Julian noticed all this happening,

"He had suddenly found an artistic flair again and realised that if he didn't get off his arse and do something it was all going to just vanish overnight."

Leslie began looking through the back catalogues for inspiration and the pieces that most held his eye were the aborted glazed range from 1974, which included 'the helmet'. He had always wanted to focus more heavily upon the glazed, sculptural ware, it was closer to his heart. It is interesting that the manganese glaze tricks the eye. You may be fooled into thinking on first glance that the 'helmet' was actually cast in bronze, a material Leslie would have loved to get a chance to work with. It must have been in his mind that he wanted a fresh start. He wanted to purge Troika of its recent past. In all of the textured ware were memories of Benny and Roland and he wanted to take back ownership of the pieces. Judith remembers,

"He really wanted to get rid of all the decorated side of it anyway he just wanted to do the smooth stuff."

Leslie was also concerned with the practical implications of Troika's work. The business needed to save money and glazing would be much less labour intensive than producing decorated texture. This would have meant that Troika did not need to employ so many staff, reducing the outgoings of the business. A lot of the firing issues which caused the high seconds rate would also be removed by having a dedicated glaze production. There would be no cross pollination from the coloured oxides.

Benny was starting his own pottery so Leslie felt justified in taking Troika in whatever direction he saw fit. The door was open to create a new sculptural line, exactly as he had wanted to in the late sixties. Leslie and Julian began to talk of the future of Troika being completely sculptural.

Left to right: Jane Fitzgerald, Louise Jinks and Alison Brigden decorating in Newlyn.

"...I had some mugs once and put 'to Hughy baby' on the bottom. I didn't put them in the kiln, Leslie did and he unpacked it and sent it off to Heal's."

Jane Fitzgerald

Unglazed prototype, c1983

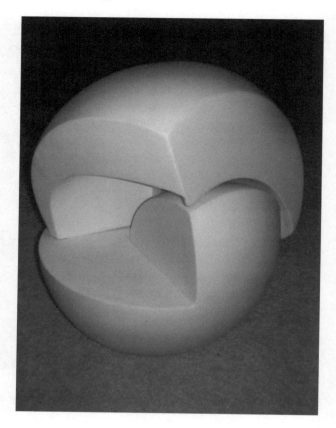

Perhaps even pieces made to limited editions rather than mass produced.

Leslie's artistic renaissance brought new focus to his work with Troika and he began to make new, complex shapes in plaster. Following the direction of the 'helmet' these new pieces began to embrace curves rather than the early square lines. Many prototypes were made that never entered production. The 'helmet' was produced again as a sculpture without the lamp fittings.

A few new pieces of square sculptural glazed ware did enter production. Including the 'floating vase', and the 'hollow square' which looks like 'The Grande Arche' in Paris.

These later pieces embraced the complexity Leslie had experimented with in the early seventies, often being cast out of two or three separate moulds and then stuck together with slip. They demonstrated his flair with sculpture and mould-making, each piece seemed to defy the laws of physics. The new pieces appeared effortless and light; confident in their white or bronze clothing.

Julian was inspired and began to create his own work in the evenings. Like Roland before him he took advantage of the open offer to use the space, the materials and Leslie's instruction. Fradgan was a good creative space to work in, quiet and ethereal with history in the walls and a modern creative industry maintained within them. It was good for Leslie to be back in that building.

Julian experienced a steep learning curve, with Leslie demanding to know why he would not follow his own instinct and find his own voice.

"I leant him a book on Picasso and there was a chapter in it where Picasso was going through a whole pile of drawing going 'real, fake, real, fake' and so on. The guy behind him said 'but you put that on the fake pile and I saw you draw that'. Picasso turned round and said 'yes even Picasso can do fakes'. Leslie loved this story, the idea that you had to put one hundred and ten percent in. You couldn't just relax. It wasn't enough to caricature what people thought you were going to do. You had to do something you felt true to."

Perhaps this story helped provide impetus for Leslie to explore sculpture once more at Troika. It brought into focus the idea that he could not call himself an artist unless he was creating exactly the work he wanted, purely for its own sake. He could not justify simply churning out objects that sold and was perhaps shocked that he had let this happen.

He insisted that Julian followed this advice in the creation of his own pieces. Leslie mentored him until he came of age by creating the 'hands' piece in 1980. The credit for this piece should go to Julian alone and so, like many other pieces, although it was made in the factory it was not part of the Troika range. Leslie was very concerned about this difference but it never stopped him from offering tools and support to those who wanted to grow artistically. Julian remembers,

"Leslie would not spare his caustic tongue as to how bad they were and why the hell was I not producing work that was about me. Why was I doing copies of what he'd done? It was only when I started producing stuff that I felt strongly about, when I was working on the hands piece that he finally agreed. He was coming up [and telling me what to do] I said 'NO, it's right that way.' He just laughed and turned around and walked off, 'Finally, you've got it!' You've got to stand your ground intellectually otherwise you aren't worth a toss. It's one of the lessons I learnt."

Leslie was enjoying total creative freedom as the partnership with Benny was finally over, after a long estrangement. They formally agreed to separate on 31st of March 1980. Benny remembers,

"When we broke up, I said to Leslie 'what do you want, the pottery or the shop?' He said he wanted Newlyn, so we went to see a solicitor and I had to raise £5000 because that was the difference in value. I kept the shop open for a while even when we weren't partners and brought some Troika off Leslie to sell in it."

Both men chose to keep their respective territories rather than close down the whole business. The factory had become synonymous with Leslie and he wanted to keep Troika going, naturally Benny kept his base. The shop was still to have exclusivity over Troika in St Ives for two more years but Benny soon sold the shop and left St Ives, there was nothing left for him there now. The gallery became a lingerie shop but is now, as with much in St Ives, a tourist merchandise emporium.

"Well I had been mumbling about it for two or three years before I left. Because we left St Ives in 1981. Sophie (his daughter), was a violinist and got a music Scholarship to Wells and Theo got a choral scholarship there... I didn't see Leslie again."

"One thing that affected him massively was the death of John Lennon. He went through a phase of doing gouaches about him."

Julian Greenwood-Penny

Troika shop window, Marazion

Leslie went back to work continually muttering how he got a raw deal. The flat and shop were saleable assets but the pottery wasn't. Leslie could have sold up too but he didn't want too. Art and Troika were more than money to him, they were his life. He turned his anger into creativity and decided he could save the ailing company.

Although they still were selling locally and to other outlets nationwide, Troika was not selling as well as it had been up to 1979. Troika would continue to supply Heal's until 1981 but in diminishing quantities. In order to progress Leslie realised that he needed to reassess Troika's selling strategy and reduce their outgoings. The major part of which was the wage bill, so when staff left in 1980 they weren't replaced. The staff who stayed were dedicated to the project of rejuvenation.

Leslie began courting Julian to become a partner in the business, he was showing some artistic promise and Leslie didn't want to lose him like he had Roland. Together they opened a new Troika shop in Marazion in 1980. It was run by Julian and sold Troika pieces, Celtic Pottery and Alan Brough's pottery. Julian remained at Fradgan Place for four days a week and went to the shop for the other three.

The only interruption to this new found hope for the future was at the end of 1980 when Leslie's hero John Lennon was shot dead in New York. A darkness passed over the world, Fradgan Place was no exception. Louise remembers,

   "I remember when John Lennon got shot, no one could believe it. I just remember the shock that went through the whole of the building, we all couldn't speak and we all felt like 'no, that's got to be not true'. I think Leslie probably just went into mourning; he went all quiet because I just don't remember hearing... I think Leslie just disappeared."

Julian watched how Leslie dealt with his grief by painting,

"One thing that affected him massively was the death of John Lennon. He went through a phase of doing gouaches about him."

Painting was still a source of solace to Leslie and Jane recalls how he was now trying to control his habit, "He was never drunk, he liked his whiskey in his coffee, but I never saw him drunk."

Meanwhile, with all the introspection and re-evaluation that was occurring, Julian had found the mould for the 'double egg-cup' hidden away in the storeroom downstairs. It had not been used in quite some time and he decided to cast one for his uncle as a birthday present. Soon the 'apple' followed and then he cast the 'fruit bowl', a large Troika 'ashtray' with bananas and apples in it. The only piece of his that made it into the Troika range.

Although Leslie was creatively focussed again designing new reliefs and pieces, Roland's moulds continued to be cast until they wore out. In order to help generate income Leslie was keen to produce as many different pieces as possible. When Julian discovered all the old moulds Leslie let them all re-enter production, reworking them as necessary. The decorators jumped on the cause, excited to be doing something that to them was brand new and may help to revitalise the business.

So from about 1980 a new wave of 'old' Troika pieces came back into production. Many pieces, such as the 'double egg-cup' or the 'apple' that had been out of production for a long time or had never even entered it, now came to the fore. This may go toward explaining the somewhat confusing history of some pieces which bear monograms from disparate periods of time.

Troika had a large back stock and with the new pieces and the new investment in time and energy there was a noticeable impact on the declining business. Against the prevailing climate of recession the total staff wages rose again in 1981, up to the same level as in 1978.

Also in 1981 Judith became pregnant. Leslie was opposed to having any more children but Judith was twelve years younger than him and convinced him otherwise. To avoid any legal difficulties they got married at the Registry Office in Penzance, witnessed by Don and Julian who remembers,

"Leslie didn't come into work that morning. Don and I went to St John's Hall, to the Registry Office, where we were witnesses to the marriage, then Leslie and Judith went home and we went back to work. I had to remember to bring a shirt in that day. Leslie turned up to work the next day."

Lawrence was born in November 1981.

Chapter Fifteen

"It was sad, sad for everyone... The end of an era."

– Jane Fitzgerald

The rejuvenation of Troika was short-lived. The graphs tell a sorry tale, in January 1982 the numbers exhibit a trend that can only be described as falling off a cliff. Almost overnight the number of staff decreases to five and the total wage bill was decimated to a third of what it was the year before. This indicates that what staff remained were now working part time. This was the beginning of the end. Troika had gone into terminal decline. Leslie's renaissance was unfortunately only to be a short-lived bubble of hope.

Although striving to keep Troika alive, forces were against him. It was becoming clear that the ramifications of the change in decade and the separation of the partnership were far-reaching and Troika would not survive forever.

Leslie's natural urge was to fight against the trend, rail against the coming of the storm. More and more old shapes were reintroduced to try and tap into past glory. He tried to combat the decline with a riot of creativity. It was the product of panic so the new pieces he made were rarely coherent or completed. Julian remembers,

"When things were going markedly downhill towards the end, Leslie did a huge pile of small glazed objects, one was a small two-piece glazed tube, very few of them were ever made, no more than two dozen. At the end, for want of a better word, he was mentally fighting to survive. He produced some very interesting work. Things like the 'wall vase', very strange things. There were a lot of trial shapes."

The 'tin mine', an uncharacteristic piece of figurative realism, emerged in 1982. It was a desperate attempt to attract the tourist market. Some of these did sell but it would never be enough to save the business. In his heart Leslie never wanted to go down the path of consumerism. He was becoming depressed at a situation he couldn't control. One that he didn't understand and ultimately one he had created. Leslie began to realise just how much work he had taken on by deciding to continue alone. Louise remembers how he just wanted to be an artist,

"I could spot the deterioration in his morale from when I started to when it started to crumble. My memory is of him being pretty low, getting frustrated at not being able to make the things that he really wanted to...he made those stupid 'tin mines'. Oh god, those were vile, we all went 'oh no please' it seemed to be sort of a desperate knee-jerk to bring in the money to support the things he wanted to make. I just remember him being low and a bit depressed really that the orders weren't coming in as they were."

Leslie desperately tried to generate some new sales; papers left from the time are covered with scribbled notes and contacts regarding potential outlets or adverts in magazines. He even contacted Heal's with some new samples to try and encourage their interest. He tried building new partnerships with shops and with people who understood the market. Including working on a set of scenic tiles with Adrian Brough, Alan's son. None of these established themselves. Leslie could never find the link between pushing sales and building relationships, he saw them as separate.

Just before the collapse, two events coincided around Christmas 1981 which brought reality into sharp focus. The birth of his new son meant that Leslie had to prioritise his new family. He had to face up to harsh reality and couldn't subsidise the business any more. Some staff had to be let go.

Then, on the 19th of December 1981 the Solomon Browne II, the Penlee lifeboat, was called out to save a distressed ship, the Union Star, whose engines had failed in heavy seas. Some of Leslie's drinking friends from the Swordfish were in the crew that day. They would not return. The lifeboat disaster affected the entire local community. There were no entries in the wage book that week. We can only assume that Leslie, who had always dreamed of being the businessman, suddenly felt that it was all for nothing. The missed week in the wage book stands as the only reminder of a sensitive man's tribute to brave local friends. Julian saw how Leslie once again turned to painting to deal with his distress,

"He was monumentally upset, after the loss of the Solomon Browne. A lot of them were friends of his. He never painted the Solomon Browne but he did paint some rather odd seascapes with monsters. But they never saw the light of day."

After the events of Christmas 1981 it is clear that Leslie lost a lot of motivation. He faced up to the truth of the situation that Troika sales were never going to return to their late seventies peak. The staff could feel the desperation. Don Fowler left that January 1982 because he wasn't being paid. Although Leslie had begun talks with Julian about becoming a partner in the business, it had become obvious that there was very little left to be a partner of. So when the shop in Marazion closed that September, after the summer season, it was never to reopen. All the old ties and familiar faces were disappearing. Leslie was nearly alone and he hated to be alone.

The momentum was such that the business managed to continue on for another year but eventually Leslie decided to cease trading. He began helping the staff to look for future employment. Julian stayed at the factory until the end of October 1983 when Leslie had secured him a job at Sunset Pottery working for Maggie Fisher. At the very end only Jane, Alison Brigden and Judith were left and Leslie made sure that they too had secured future employment. On the final day Leslie thanked them for their efforts and gave them a carnation. It was all he had left. The doors finally closed in November 1983.

After twenty tumultuous years Troika was finally over. Due to the suddenness of the collapse there is a suggestion that Leslie had been hiding the true extent of Troika's lack of income. He was living in the hope that it was a short-term blip, that sales would return. The business closed with an overdraft approaching £20000, an exorbitant sum in 1983. There was barely enough left for Leslie to survive on for a few months. He had personally been funding the business; most of this debt had accumulated through Leslie paying the staff for those extra few years.

It is easy to think that Leslie's drinking was the largest factor in the demise of Troika. Although a valid concern, this analysis is too simple. Troika was successful for the majority of its long twenty-year history. This was a history where alcohol was always present and had no doubt played its part in celebrating the early success. We have also seen how, although he continued to drink, Leslie experienced a renaissance in the late 1970's and began devoting more care and time to Troika with noticeable effect. It was five more years before the business closed, too long to consider only one factor.

One of the defining factors of Troika's lengthy success was their ability to adapt to changing tastes. A decade earlier when confronted by the environmental and economic changes at the end of the sixties, Troika changed to textured ware and flourished in the new decade. They did this organically with Leslie and Benny naturally complimenting the trends of the time. In the sixties and the seventies they were part of the times and at one with their environment. Maria, Leslie's friend remembers how Leslie had never lost the vernacular of his youth,

"He used to say 'do you dig' all the time. It was very much of the sixties but he never lost it. He just went on saying it. He would constantly tell you something, he'd go banging on and banging on and then he'd say 'do ya' dig?'"

By 1980 Troika was a decade away from the new youth. What was once innovative and relevant soon became staid and passé. Where they were seers in the sixties, they had become the establishment in the seventies and now for the first time Troika was out of date.

Crucial to this loss of impetus was Benny leaving. Without Benny there was no direction, no drive to maintain production and fill the orders that rolled in.

> *"[Leslie] used to say 'do you dig' all the time. It was very much of the sixties but he never lost it. He just went on saying it. He would constantly tell you something, he'd go banging on and banging on and then he'd say 'do ya' dig?'"*
>
> *Maria Heitel*

Creativity requires an outlet and Benny was always able to find one. He was always able to put Troika on the shelves of local, national and international shops. He was able to guide the production process to ensure that the pieces that were being made were the pieces he could sell. He kept an eye upon the wild impulses of his own and Leslie's creations in order to make them palatable to the public. A public which the business relied upon to generate income. Without this communication, the creativity which emerged from Troika in the final years, such as the new sculptural ware, became tragically irrelevant, regardless of its quality. The pieces that emerged were never made in large enough quantities to dominate production and it seemed to the public that Troika had lost some of its genesis. With the re-introduction of past shapes, it also looked like Troika had begun to rely upon past glory which detracted from any progression it had made.

When Benny left, Troika had neither salesman nor shop. Troika had started well with both partners contributing equally to both elements of the business, design and sales. It flourished when their roles were naturally defined and became separate. When Benny left it was too much for one person to do alone, regardless of their temperament. Leslie found it difficult to maintain the contacts that had been established. These contacts had slowly ebbed away. Julian describes their relationship,

   "Benny was the piece of sand in the oyster that creates the pearl. He was the irritation that got Leslie off his bum sometimes. That's why they were a team. Benny was the trier; he would go and try things. Before he met Leslie he had god knows how many jobs. But the ability to not give up but just keep fighting and do whatever was necessary was Benny's half of it. It was Benny's, not business brain, but impetus that connected with Leslie's talent. The nearest thing I can acquaint it to is Gilbert and George, you need both of them. That is why it was Troika."

It was prudent to start with internal factors within the business that contributed to the demise of Troika. However, there were many mitigating external factors resulting from the economic climate of the early eighties. These cannot be ignored.

In 1979, VAT increased from 8% to 15%. As with many businesses Troika could not pass this increase on to its customers so had to absorb it. This virtually obliterated their already diminishing profit margin due to the inflation of the seventies. It sent a shock-wave through the business. Profit margins were tight at Troika anyway, due to the time-consuming production process and high seconds' ratio.

The economic wind was changing and thousands of miles away, in factories across the globe, new entrepreneurs were grabbing onto the coat-tails of the manufacturing revolution. New products made from new materials, made by cheap, efficient manufacturing processes were saturating the shops. They may have had little in the way of soul but they had style in abundance.

Much of the UK manufacturing base suffered at this time. In a cruel pincer movement the UK was not only more expensive to produce in but consequently overrun by cheap imports. Troika had always trodden a fine line between exclusivity and availability but now this market was crushed by these new products. With a general tightening of the belt in the early eighties, the predominant factor determining choice became price not quality. Especially when these new goods mimicked quality so well.

The local market was also undergoing a period of change. Alan Brough remembers that many retailers along the south coast who would stock pottery or sculpture began to change their buying strategy. They began asking to take goods on 'sale or return' placing the risk squarely with the producer rather than themselves. At the same time Troika began to find it harder to collect the money for orders paid on receipt of goods. In 1982 they introduced a five percent discount for payment within seven days.

This change in attitude emerged as the tourist market in the South West dried up. Package holidays had grown in popularity during the mid seventies. Now it was cheaper to fly to Spain for some guaranteed sun and a warm Mediterranean sea rather than risk the sporadic onset of mist and freezing waters of Cornwall or the south coast. When Troika lost the Heal's contract and had to rely heavily on local sales, they were over-exposed to a market that had contracted. Even those who did brave the UK summer and wanted a souvenir rarely checked the bottom of a piece to see where it was made. Now, in these leaner times, if they found something in a shop in a seaside town at the right price and that they liked, then they weren't concerned with provenance or quality.

In Newlyn, Troika was not the only business to suffer. Leaper Pottery, run by Eric Leaper, who was as famous for his parties as his pots, closed in 1980. Celtic Pottery became Sunset Pottery in the late seventies and finally closed in 1984. Tremaen Pottery had a shop in Penzance as well as a workshop by the slip in Newlyn. They struggled through the recession but were forced to close the workshop in 1988. Even the ineffable Alan Brough brought his son in to help him produce more pots in 1985 but had moved out of Newlyn by 1990. It was all gone.

In this light it is a wonder Troika survived as long as it did, finally closing in 1983 Troika was not only out of style but of out luck.

Chapter Sixteen

"It used to be lovely watching Leslie, it just flowed, he knew what he was doing. I would be waiting for him and he'd say, 'I'll just do the top side of the mould and then we can go.'"

– Judith Illsley

Leslie working on a relief c1963

Leslie had first tried to sell the business in October 1983. A couple of young potters tried to buy it to start up a pottery but the bank wouldn't lend them the £27,000 needed to buy it. That era was over. So Leslie tried simply to sell the building and the plant. The machinery was worth nothing and in the end they had to pay someone to take it away. In 1986 the building was finally sold for £21,000 and was eventually turned into flats. The money cleared all of the debts but there was little left. Everything was back where it had once begun, an empty landscape, as if nothing had ever been there at all.

When they cleared the building, most of the paperwork and records were thrown away. The primary evidence left today, such as the wage book, was only salvaged through Judith's presence of mind. She cleared some of the shelves in the office into a box and told Leslie, "You're not touching these." She might have been the only person he ever listened to. Troika was dead to Leslie but Judith was still incredibly proud of her husband and his achievements. She remains fiercely protective to this day.

In this time of termination and catharsis, Leslie made a small decision that had massive repercussions today. The business had been taken off the market but when cash was offered for the moulds, he agreed. Leslie was desperate for money and also sold all the unglazed biscuit ware that was left. He was quite amazed that anyone would want them at all.

At least three groups of people bought the moulds. Some were put into storage in a barn at Carnyorth but disappeared when a mineshaft opened up, swallowing half the barn and moulds. But the others are still extant. At the time Judith berated him for this, she thought the moulds should have been destroyed. But he brushed aside her concerns because he considered that they were only relics. He had not sold the business or the name. The new owners of the moulds couldn't use the name 'Troika'. Judith states,

"Leslie never sold the business, he sold the moulds and he sold the property but he never sold the business so I still hold the copyright on that."

After all of the turmoil of the closure of Fradgan Place, the birth of Rachael in July 1984, three days after Leslie's birthday, was a welcome blessing. It was supposed to herald the start of a new era for the family. A calmer life, bringing up their two young children together.

Soon after Rachael was born she had to spend a lot of time in hospital, Judith went with her leaving Leslie at home. In her absence he was knocked down by a motorbike and broke his arm. Suddenly the whole family was in hospital. Lawrence went to join Judith and Rachael in Treliske Hospital on the outskirts of Truro. Leslie was a few miles away in the old City Hospital, which used to be in the centre of Truro. He was put onto what he called 'the motorbike wing', next to lots of broken young men. He had some beer brought in and they were all smoking and drinking on the ward.

When the family finally returned home it was time to move out for good. With the business gone, there was no major source of income so they were forced to downsize. As they were moving into a smaller house a lot of their belongings had to be sold, thrown away or put into storage. Leslie put most of the Troika pieces they had into a skip. Rarities, one-offs, prototypes, 'Sculptures for Living' pieces, reliefs, as well as major pieces of sculpture went into this skip. Judith managed to salvage a few pieces but not many.

Who could have known how valuable these pieces were to become? At the time Troika was practically worthless; you couldn't even give it away. The only value it retained was a harsh reminder of strife and failure. Leslie hated them as you can only hate something you have created and once passionately loved. He was destroying the part of himself that had been rejected by the world and it was now too painful for even him to keep hold of it.

Leslie had spent nearly all of his adult life with Benny, building and maintaining Troika. Now he was at a loss of what to do. Although he had rediscovered painting, he was suffering from depression. We shouldn't underestimate the scale of the psychological impact the collapse of Troika would have had on him. As harsh a critic on himself as he was on others. He felt like a failure. Judith remembers,

"At the end he was upset because he said 'well that's just twenty odd-years just gone down the plughole."

With a young family to support he tried to find work but resented having to go to the local Job Centre in Penzance. Maggie Fisher who had run Celtic Pottery had now opened a restaurant called the Bay Tree Restaurant in Penzance. Leslie asked her for a job washing the dishes. She refused. She claims that she just couldn't bear to see a talented man like Leslie doing such menial work.

"At the end he was upset because he said 'well that's just twenty-odd years just gone down the plughole.'"

Judith Illsley

What followed was something of a conspiracy. It remains a rumour but the idea that such a project was even considered shows how much esteem and respect Leslie was held in by those who knew him. Many of those who were potentially involved shall remain in the shadows but the story goes that a small group got together to help Leslie continue as an artist. Each week he would go to see his old friend Tony Sanders in his gallery on Chapel Street in Penzance. Each week he went with a painting, had a glass of whiskey and a chat with Tony and left without the painting. He didn't get much for each one but it was something to live off. It did more than that, it also kept his pride intact.

Leslie painted a lot in the years after Troika. He had a little shed in the back garden. He not only displayed them in Tony Sander's gallery, but in the New Craftsman Gallery in St Ives. Also in true Leslie style they could be found in many of the local pubs and restaurants. He preferred to paint abstract paintings but often turned his hand to more commercial subjects such as nudes, character studies, horses or musicians. Versatile to the last. He preferred gouache or watercolour paints to oils, so he could paint quickly, as inspiration took him.

The family was coming to terms with the future, Lawrence had started school, Rachael was healthy. Then, not long after the dust had settled on the Troika story with the final sale of the building, Leslie found a lump in his neck.

It turned out to be cancerous. He had radio-therapy at Derriford Hospital near Plymouth.

The end of Troika in late 1983 was only supposed to be the end of Troika as a manufacturer. When Leslie ceased trading he did so in order to save Troika from bankruptcy. It was the intention to sell off the assets and then begin trading again but with a much scaled-down operation. Leslie wanted to produce exclusively sculptural glazed ware, perhaps even on his own. It took him a couple of years to recover from the emotional impact of the perceived failure of his life's work and look to the future. But by then he was ill.

Louise went to see him during his illness and found him painting, "I just remember when he was really poorly and dying and I went out to see him in his little studio shed in the back garden, Christ it was so moving, it was like he knew his time was limited and he was just like pumping out work like he couldn't stop. Fantastic really, inspiring and sad."

Judith forced him to sign these paintings and his back catalogue by way of establishing a heritage. Much of his prodigious output now lies quietly waiting to be discovered.

He spent the last eight weeks of his life in bed visited by a few friends. Alan sometimes stopped by with some whiskey. It was a slow death and his home became his hospice, Judith looking after him right up to the end and remembers that he still would talk about the future of the venture that had occupied nearly half of his life. He died in his sleep in 1989 and was laid to rest in Pendeen Church Cemetery overlooking the sea. His headstone reads "Do not go gentle into that good night." He never wanted to get old.

There was a small funeral and many people didn't even know he had died. Benny returned to Cornwall many years later and was shocked to find out,

"Leslie was dead by the time I went back. I heard about it. I could just not understand why no-one told me that there was a funeral. Judith didn't want anyone to know."

Roland remembers, "I was really shocked when I found out he died. It affected me quite profoundly. I looked upon him as a kind of older brother for sure. I missed him when I left I felt really sad. Yeah it was a family, they were interesting times."

Suddenly Judith was all alone with two young children. It became the sad truth that with his death none of his four children would ever get to know the man they had heard other people talk about. Leslie himself died without knowing of the legacy he had left. He missed all of the renewed interest in Troika which came in the mid-nineties and he died feeling under-appreciated and like a failure.

"Leslie had this brilliant idea way back in St Ives, he used to say to me, in about thirty or forty years time your service will be valuable, people will pay you to help them spend their time. He had this big idea that what we were doing then would help people in the future connect with creativity and that's what's kind of happened. He wanted it in people's homes not in museums, that's for sure."

"He had this big idea that what we were doing then would help people in the future connect with creativity and that's what's kind of happened. He wanted it in people's homes not in museums, that's for sure."

Roland Bence

Troika selection, including a piece from the 'Sculptures for Living' range.

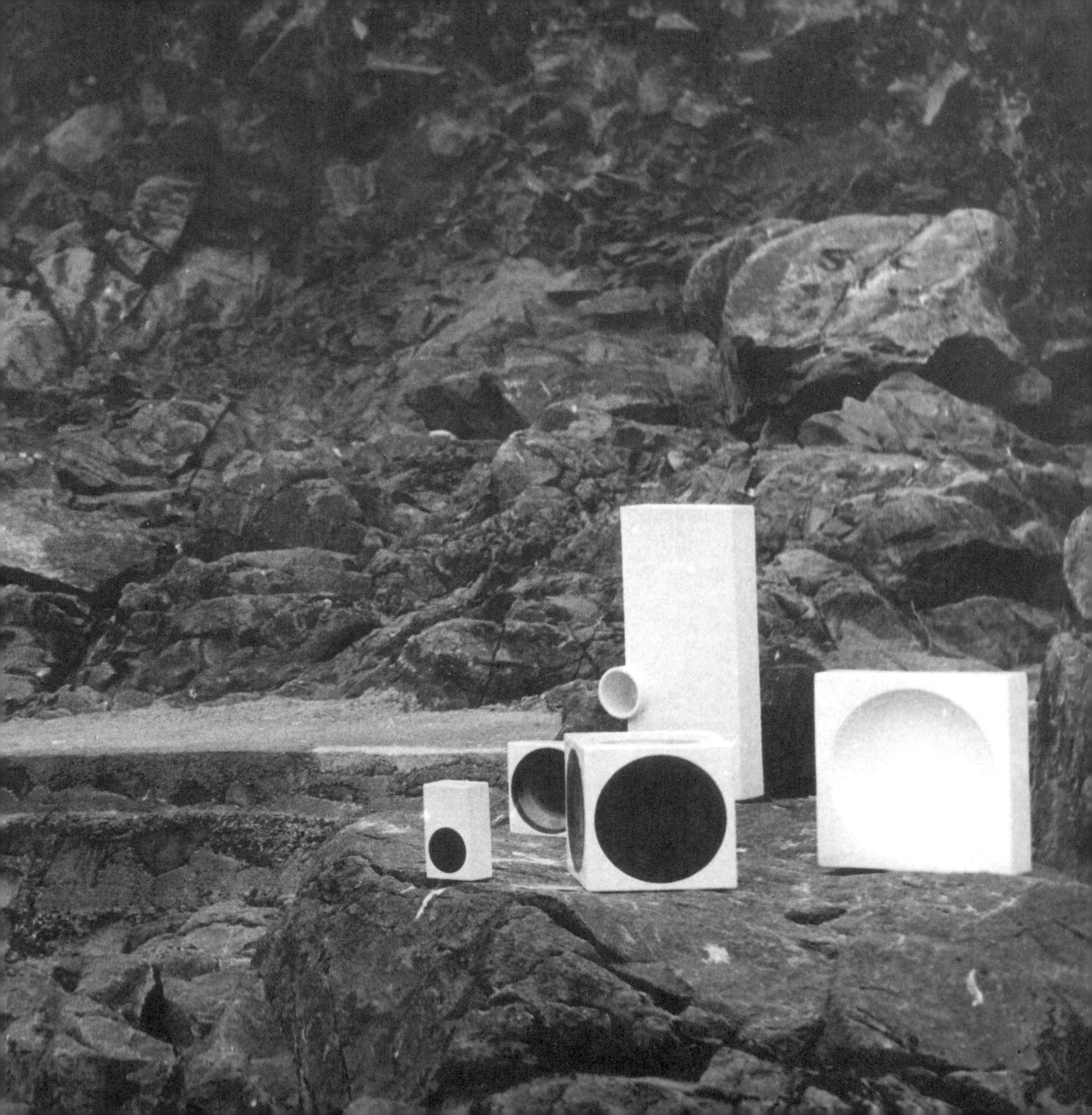

Credits

Introduction
Photograph of Benny Sirota courtesy of Judith Illsley

Chapter One
23, 24, 26–27 Photographs courtesy of Judith Illsley

Chapter Two
30, 32, 34–35, 41 Photographs courtesy of Judith Illsley
36 Collection of Richard Wheatley*

Chapter Three
45 Collection of Ben Harris*
46, 47, 49 Photographs courtesy of Judith Illsley

Chapter Four
53, 54, 57 Photographs courtesy of Judith Illsley

Chapter Five
61, 65 Photographs courtesy of Judith Illsley

Chapter Six
73 Photograph courtesy of Judith Illsley
77 Photography courtesy of Teresa Foley

Chapter Seven
81, 82, 83, 85 Photographs courtesy of Judith Illsley
84 Austin Reed Gallery Exhibition flyer courtesy of Mary Lambert and The Marjorie Parr Gallery
90 Collection of Benny Sirota**

Chapter Eight
96, 101 Collection of Benny Sirota**

Chapter Ten
110 Photograph of sketch courtesy of Judith Illsley
114, 115 Collection of Richard Wheatley*
117 Collection of Ben Harris*

Chapter Eleven
120 Collection of Ben Harris*

Chapter Twelve
128, 129 Collection of Penlee House Gallery*
130 Photograph by Ben Harris
131 Collection of Benny Sirota**

Chapter Thirteen
137, 138 Photographs courtesy of Avril Machray
139 Photograph courtesy of Judith Illsley

Chapter Fourteen
149 Photograph courtesy of Judith Illsley
150 Photograph by Ben Harris
152 Photograph courtesy of Julian Greenwood-Penny

Chapter Sixteen
161, 166–167 photography courtesy of Judith Illsley

Colour insert images

1. Collection of Richard Wheatley*
2. Collection of Benny Sirota**
3. Collection of Benny Sirota**
4. Photograph courtesy of Judith Illsley
5. Collection of Richard Wheatley*
6. Collection of Ben Harris*
7. Photograph courtesy of Judith Illsley
8. Collection of Richard Wheatley*
9. Courtesy of Colin Richards and Teresa Bretherton
10. Photograph courtesy of Judith Illsley
11. Courtesy of Colin Richards and Teresa Bretherton
12. Collection of Ben Harris*
13. Photographs courtesy of Judith Illsley
14. Collection of Ben Harris*
15. Courtesy of Colin Richards and Teresa Bretherton
16. Collection of Richard Wheatley*
17. Collection of Ben Harris*
18. Collection of Richard Wheatley*
19. Collection of Richard Wheatley*
20. Collection of Ben Harris*
21. Photograph courtesy of Judith Illsley
22. Collection of Ben Harris*
23. Collection of Richard Wheatley*
24. Photograph courtesy of Judith Illsley
25. Collection of Ben Harris*
26. Courtesy of Colin Richards and Teresa Bretherton
27. Courtesy of Colin Richards and Teresa Bretherton
28. Collection of Richard Wheatley*
29. Collection of Ben Harris*

*Photography by Amy Willoughby
**Photography by Theo Sirota

Index

A

B

C

D

E

F

G

H

I

K

L

M

M

N

O

P

R

S

T

V

W

Y

Z